THE GROVE OF DANA

Druid Course

NEW ORDER OF DRUIDS

DRUID COURSE

Published by Lulu.com
ISBN: 978-1-365-48183-3

Photo cover from istockphoto.com

Druid Course, by Maya St. Clair, edited by Elke Thomas - Copyright 2010 - 2011 Druidcircle.net. All rights reserved.

First edition 2016 – Lulu.com

Ogmios be at your right hand, guiding your way.
Rosmerta be at your left hand, guiding your way.
Cernunnos open your mind, and the Mothers keep you safe,
as you begin the great Adventure of Learning.

      - Adapted from a book of Pagan prayers
        by Ceswir Serith

Contents

Walking the Druid Path:
An Introduction to the Druid Course

Welcome seekers to the last of the basic courses of the New Order of Druids. To get to this course you had to search into yourself and into mythology in both the Bard and Ovate courses. Druid is not something you just become; it takes years of study and dedication. The ancient druids took 20 years to become Druids; most programs available now are only 3 years long. This course is only to give you an introduction to your chosen path, whether you continue on with your studies after this course is completely up to you.

The Druid course is different. It is all about the practical side of your path. It is our hope that by the time you finish the course you will have a well-defined personal practice and a foot on the Druid Path. By the very end of it you will have an outline of your religious worldview, a working knowledge of what a ritual is, the Celtic Wheel of the year, and how to set up your own sacred space, Celtic Shamanism, and divination among other things. You will also be expected to start a Druid Journal, which will serve as one of your final projects.

This is just a suggestion but it might be beneficial to buy a book called A Pagan Book of Prayer by Ceisiwr Serith. It has god so many prayers for so many different occasions.

CHAPTER ONE

Uhat is Religion?

It is obvious to anyone who follows the news that religion has a huge impact on our world today. However, ask anyone to define religion and you will probably get a different answer from each person you ask. Each person could have their favorite definition, which they think is the correct one and sometimes, if not most times, this definition is not complete. Basically, there is no consensus on the definition of religion.

Etymology of the word religion changes depending on the time the etymology was used. In the fifth century Cicero said that the word religion came from relegare, which means go through again or read again, from (re) meaning again and (legere) meaning read. And in the eleventh century the word religion was thought to come from Anglo-French religiun, from Old French religion meaning religious community, from Latin religionem, which means respect for what is sacred, reverence for the Gods. In popular etymology among the later ancients and many modern writers religion is connected to religare, to bind fast, to the notion of place an obligation on or bond between humans and Gods. Another possible origin is religiens, which means careful.[1]

Most people focus on a very narrow definition that matches the individual's own religion, but few others. Some definitions exclude beliefs and practices, like for example a required belief in a God or Goddess or a combination of both and this will exclude religions like Buddhism and some forms of religious Satanism. Some definitions are so broad that they include beliefs and areas of study that most people do not regard as religion. And some definitions use terms in them that in and of themselves require further defining.[2]

Now let me give you some definitions that are out there for religion.

Wikipedia defines religion as a set of beliefs concerning the cause, nature, and purpose of the universe, especially when considered as the creation of a supernatural agency or agencies, usually involving devotional and ritual observances, and often containing a moral code governing the conduct of human affairs.[3]

The American Heritage Dictionary gives us four definitions of religion. Religion is a belief in and reverence for a supernatural power or powers regarded as creator and governor of the universe and a personal or institutionalized system grounded in such belief and worship; the life or condition of a person in a religious order; a set of beliefs, values, and practices based on the teachings of a spiritual leader. And finally a cause, principle, or activity pursued with zeal or conscientious devotion.[4]

Barnes and Noble (Cambridge) Encyclopedia (1990) say no single definition will suffice to encompass the varied sets of traditions, practices, and ideas, which constitute different religions.

The Concise Oxford Dictionary (1990) says human recognition of superhuman controlling power and especially of a personal God entitled to obedience.[5]

Then of course there are the definitions put forward by people who are formulating the theories of religion. The different approaches to studying religion give us the different theories of religion. It is also interesting to note that the same people who gave us theories on culture, society, mythology, economy and politics are the same ones that gave us the theories of religion.

Theories of religion can be divided into theories that focus on what religion is and theories that focus on what it does.[6] I don't want to go into too much detail on theories of religion but I will give you the definitions put forward by the most famous people on the field.

Edward Burnett Taylor defined religion as belief in spiritual beings. He believed that all religious ideas developed out of a primitive belief in the animate nature of natural phenomena or animism. For Taylor all religion is a mistaken attempt to make sense of the physical world in which we live.

Émile Durkheim saw society rather than the individual as the source of both the profane and the sacred. To him religion is the embodiment of society's highest goals and ideals. Religion acts as a cohesive social force and adds up to more than the sum of its parts.

Clifford Geertz saw religion as a system of symbols which acts to establish powerful, pervasive and long-lasting moods and motivations in men by formulating concepts of a general order of existence and clothing these concepts with such an aura of factuality that the moods and motivations seem uniquely realistic.

Malinowski focused on the individual, psychological function of religion. For him religion came out of a response to emotional stress. When technical knowledge failed, humans turned to magic and religion in order to achieve their ends.[7]

Karl Marx saw everything in terms of economics. He saw religion originating from alienation and that it is there to keep the masses happy with economic inequality. It was a dependent value, mostly on economics.

James George Frazer believed that magic came before religion. As magic failed people looked for other psychological support and concocted the illusion that spiritual beings could help them.

Max Weber didn't focus on the truth claims of religions so much as what their role was in society and though he agreed with Durkheim's definition, unlike Durkheim, he thought that religion could be a force of change in society.

Sigmund Freud saw religion as an illusion. Freud thought that religion was something that people really wanted to believe in and was a response to repression.

Mircea Eliade saw religion as something special and autonomous that cannot be reduced to social, economical or psychological alone. He also differentiated between the sacred and the profane.

Carl Gustav Jung saw religion as psychological phenomena, and a natural process, which stems from archetypes in the human mind. He thought it performs the function of harmonizing the psyche and also a beneficial phenomenon.[8]

When looking at different religions there are some things that seem to be common to all. Most, if not all religions have beliefs, sacred texts and writings, rituals and ceremonies, and some sort of moral code or ethics. I'll discuss characteristic separately.

Beliefs:
People who follow a religion have a specific belief about deity, doctrines and/or creeds, theology and sacred stories and myths. Sometimes they have beliefs in all of these or just a few of them depending on the religion.

Sacred Texts and Writings:
Sacred texts and writings are very easy to define in religions like Islam, where they have the Qur'an, in Christianity where they have the Bible, and in Judaism, where they have the Torah (Old Testament), but what about paganism? Sacred texts and writings can come in three forms; oral traditions, which are then written down later, artistic representations like statues, paintings, and icons, and manuscripts like the ones mentioned above or writings of the influential persons in any religion.

Rituals and Ceremonies:
Almost every religion has its rituals and ceremonies; these include festivals to mark the seasons and important events, sacrifice and/or offerings, sacramental rites, pilgrimages, meditation, healing rites and customary worship.

Ethics:
Every religion has a code of ethics and moral standards that it lives by. These codes and standards are influenced by the religion and the culture the individual may come from. What is acceptable in one culture may not be so in another. And religion is most certainly influenced by the culture it lives in, just like it influences that culture.

What sorts of religions are there? When people ask the above question the first answers that are given are Christianity, Islam, Judaism, Buddhism, Paganism, and so on. There are three religions from what is mentioned above that are the same SORT of religion. Christianity, Islam and Judaism are all monotheistic. There are even forms of Buddhism and Hinduism that are considered monotheistic while others are considered polytheistic, but what do those terms mean? I will be defining the sorts of religions available next.

Monotheism comes from the Greek mono meaning single or alone and theos meaning a god.[9] So monotheism is the doctrine or belief that there is only one God.[10]

Polytheism from French polythéisme (16th century), formed from Greek poly-theos "of many Gods", from polys "many" and theos "god".[11] Polytheism then is the doctrine of or belief in more than one god or in many Gods.[12]

These two terms are the most well known of all the sorts of religions out there but there are more.

Knowing that no definition is perfect, the best way to describe religion is to use the following: "Religion is any specific system of belief about deity, often involving rituals, a code of ethics, a philosophy of life and a world view."[13]

Endnotes

1 "Etymology of Religion" November 2001. Access Date: February 12, 2010
<http://www.etymonline.com/index.php?term=religion>

2 "Definitions of the word 'Religion'" Access date: February 9, 2010
<http://www.religioustolerance.org/rel_defn.htm>

3 "Religion" February 13, 2010 Access date: February 13, 2010
<http://en.wikipedia.org/wiki/Religion>

4 "Religion" The American Heritage Dictionary of the English Language, Fourth Edition. Houghton Mifflin Company, 2004. February 13, 2010 <Dictionary.com http://dictionary.reference.com/browse/Religion>

5 "Definitions of the word 'Religion'" Access date: February 9, 2010
<http://www.religioustolerance.org/rel_defn.htm>

6 "Theories of Religion" February 5, 2010 Access date: February 12, 2010
<http://en.wikipedia.org/wiki/Theories_of_religion>

7 Robert A. Segal. The Blackwell Companion to the Study of Religion (Massachusetts: Blackwell Publishing, 2006) pp. 3-24

8 "Theories of Religion" February 5, 2010 Access date: February 17, 2010 <http://en.wikipedia.org/wiki/Theories_of_religion>

9 "Monotheism." Online Etymology Dictionary. Douglas Harper, Historian. 17 Feb. 2010. <Dictionary.com http://dictionary.reference.com/browse/Monotheism>.

10 "Monotheism." The American Heritage® Dictionary of the English Language, Fourth Edition. Houghton Mifflin Company, 2004. 17 Feb. 2010. <Dictionary.com http://dictionary.reference.com/browse/Monotheism>.

11 "polytheism." Online Etymology Dictionary. Douglas Harper, Historian. 17 Feb. 2010. <Dictionary.com http://dictionary.reference.com/browse/polytheism>.

12 "polytheism." Dictionary.com Unabridged. Random House, Inc. 17 Feb. 2010. <Dictionary.com http://dictionary.reference.com/browse/polytheism>.

13 "Definitions of the word "Religion" Access date: February 9, 2010 <http://www.religioustolerance.org/rel_defn.htm>

CHAPTER TWO
What is Paganism?

Now that you know what a religion is, it is time to figure out what Paganism is as well, since most people love labels and really expect them. Paganism (Neo-Paganism) is an umbrella term that describes a variety of denominations called by pagan traditions. They vary in beliefs and practices, and though that is a source of pride for pagans it can be confusing to others. In Paganism you can find many traditions like: Asatru, Ceremonial Magick, Celtic, Druidry, Santeria, Voudon, Shamanism, Eclectic, Solitary, Wicca, Family Traditions, and Blended just to name a few.

General Characteristics of Paganism:

1. Paganism is a religion.
2. Paganism is a modern religion that borrows from old concepts and practices.
3. Paganism has no central hierarchy and/or dogma.
4. Paganism stresses personal responsibility
5. Paganism offers a different Worldview
6. Paganism is a spirituality.
7. The law in most countries protects paganism under the laws of freedom of religion.
8. Paganism stresses the interconnectedness of all things.[1]

Definition of Paganism:

"The word "pagan" (small "p") is often used pejoratively to mean simply "uncivilized", or even "un-Christian" (the two generally being assumed identical), in the same way that "heathen" is used. Its literal meaning is "rural", from the countryside (pagus)."

In the book A History of Pagan Europe, the authors gave the following criteria for a religion to be called Paganism. "They are polytheistic, recognizing a plurality of divine beings, which may or may not be avatars or other aspects of underlying unity/duality/trinity etc. They view nature as a theophany, a manifestation of divinity, not as a "fallen" creation of the latter. They recognize the female divine principle, called the Goddess (with a capital "G" to distinguish her from the many particular goddesses), as well as, or instead of the male divine principle, the God."

In our world today, a lot of people are familiar with the general definition of what paganism is and they call themselves pagan based on that definition. Little is known about the criteria set by the authors of The History of Pagan Europe, which I feel gives an accurate and much more rounded idea of what Paganism is. Most of the people who call themselves pagan today would probably fit into the criteria set by the authors.[2]

The main Principles of Paganism are as follows:

1. You are responsible for the beliefs you chose to adopt.
2. You are responsible for your own actions and your spiritual and personal development.
3. Everything is sacred.

Groups will add more to these principles as fitting with their own traditions. This will bring us to the Celtic Religion. The next chapter will discuss what it is and what we really know of it.

Endnotes

1 Joyce Higginbotham. Paganism: An Introduction to Earth- Centered Religions (New York: Llewellyn 2002)

2 Nigel Pennick and Joyce Jones. A History of Pagan Europe. (New York: Routledge 2007) pp. 1-2

CHAPTER THREE

What is Celtic Religion and What Do We Really Know About It?

In the previous two chapters we laid down a foundation for what we came here (to the druid course) to really do and that is to study the Celtic religion. So the first question we need to ask is what is Celtic religion? The immediate and simple answer is it is the religion followed by the Celtic peoples. The next question would be what and how much do we really know about it, when we know that the Celts didn't leave behind any written records? Another simple answer would be surprisingly quite a bit more than most people realize.

This chapter will take us beyond the simple answers to the above questions and will give us a look into the components of the Celtic religion, and the sources we have for these components.

What are the sources?

Contrary to what most people think there are many sources for the Celtic religion, however, none of them can stand on their own. If you take them all together you can get a pretty good general picture of what the religion entailed.

The sources can be divided into three categories. The first is direct or near direct evidence (main sources), the second is evidence that we can use but is not very helpful (secondary sources), and the third is evidence from other Indo-European (IE) cultures. The IE cultures are the ancestors to half the population of the world.

The first main source is the archeological evidence of the Celts. As sources go this is the only direct source we have on the pre-historic Celtic religion. This evidence includes things like sacred sites (Tara, Emain Macha etc...), objects found at known Celtic sites (objects that are left as offerings at wells, or river mouths, the Coligny Calendar, etc...), and the burial sites (and that includes bog bodies).

The second main source is the Insular records. Even though Christians wrote them, they were still written close enough to the time when the Insular Celts were Pagan for them to retain most of the important information needed. These Insular records include early British histories, sociopolitical geographies and the Irish and Welsh tales.

The third main source is the Classical writings. These are the writings of Romans and Greeks who were contemporary to the Celts. Keep in mind though, that these writers were biased, because of their conflicts with the Celts, their knowledge, their politics, and the audiences these writings are geared towards.

The first of the secondary sources is inscriptions. Most of the inscriptions came from the Roman era. They include place names, and names of gods and goddesses.

The second secondary source is the folk traditions. These folk traditions are from countries that are considered "Celtic". Those folk traditions are still showing their Pagan origins.

The final source I want to talk about is one that will perhaps help people following the Celtic religion fill in the gaps left by all the evidence we have. That final source is comparative studies. By looking at linguistics, comparative IE studies, comparative religious studies and general histories of the IE cultures we can try to provide explanations and possible fills for the unknown gaps that are left.[1]

What do we know about the Celtic Religion?

Let us look back at the components of religion from the first chapter. The components are as follows: beliefs, sacred texts and/or writings, rituals and ceremonies and ethics. For the rest of this chapter we will look at each of the components and talk generally on what we know of each.

Let us start with belief in the gods. It is apparent from most of the evidence found so far that there are three phases of development when it comes to the worship of the Gods.

The first phase is the Pre-Roman phase. The features of that time are that there were no statues of the Celtic gods and no permanent buildings for worship. They were worshipped in nature and were not confined in a closed space. The Celts, when invading the Romans and Greeks, laughed at the statues of the Gods because they were depicted as human beings.

The second phase is when the influence of the Greeks and Romans first appeared, through interactions of war and trading, which was going on between the cultures. Some Roman and Greek gods were brought back by the Celts and were worshipped alongside the Celtic gods, sometimes these gods were associated with each other and became one and the same. This is the time when the first iconography and epithets are found.

The third and final phase is when the Romans conquered the Celts and their religious influence also appeared more prominently. Some religious houses were built and from this time we find some statues of the gods and goddesses as well as iconography and epithets.

The Celts were very religious; they saw gods everywhere and that is evident from the large number of god names found. There are at least 400 god-names recorded, 300 of which only appear once. This has two implications; the first is that the Celts had tribal gods that were worshipped by a specific tribe and not any other and the second is that the names were really just different names for the same gods, for example, Brigit could be Brigit as well as the Exalted One. They were also very superstitious which can be evident from the fact that they have a calendar for when to do things.

As you study the different gods you will notice that while most of the gods had certain functions that were dominant, the Celtic gods were not specialized. For example, some goddesses were fertility goddesses as well as war goddesses and mother goddesses.[2]

While people following the Celtic religion don't have any sacred texts they do have the myths, and folklore. These writings can give us information on the gods, rituals and social behavior.

The Celtic religion has four great seasonal feasts, Samhain, Imbolc, Beltane, and Lughnasadh. There is also some evidence for name-giving ceremonies, rituals to be accepted into a warrior band, initiation to kingship rituals, death rituals, divinatory rituals, curative rituals, collection of plants rituals, blessings and curses, and temple unroofing rituals.

The Celts had a code of ethics, which is very evident from the laws handed down to us in the Irish records. They had codes and laws that governed everything from hospitality to how to treat a sick person.

In the coming chapters I will be discussing some of these components in greater detail.

Endnotes

1 "Celtic Religion What Information Do We Really Have?" Draeconin's Pagan Info. Access Date: March 7, 2010. http://draeconin.com/database/celtreli.htm

2 Miranda Green. The Gods of the Celts (Great Britain: Sutton Publishing, 2004)

CHAPTER FOUR

Choosing Your Path

Now that you have learned the very basic building blocks of the Celtic religion it is time to personalize your chosen path. You may be wondering what I am talking about exactly; well, in the Celtic religion there are many different pantheons. There are the Irish, Welsh, Gaulish, Breton, etc… and it is sometimes hard to decide how to begin your journey.

For now let us establish one basic principle. Choose a single pantheon and stick to it for the reminder of the course. You will see that some deities can cross lines of cultures but each culture has its own customs and style of honoring/worshipping deity. When you try to mix the different deities things can get confusing. You would have to learn the different names and customs and mythologies associated with each culture and that is quite a lot!

If you aren't sure which path you want to follow or have an interest in a few of them read a little more on each culture (use the online mythologies which you can find on www.sacred-texts.com), one of them will speak to you more than the others. Also here are some resources that you might like to know about:

Some Irish Resources:
- Tales of the Elders of Ireland translated by Ann Dooley and Harry Roe
- Early Irish Myths and Legends by Jeffery Gantz
- Irish Myths and Legends by Lady Augusta Gregory
- Gods and Fighting Men by Lady Augusta Gregory
- The Tain by Ciaran Carson

Some Welsh Resources:
- The Mabinogi and Other Medieval Welsh Tales - Patrick K. Ford
- British Goblins: Welsh Folklore, Fairy Mythology, Legends and Traditions - Wirt Sikes
- The Four Ancient Books of Wales - William F. Skene
- Celtic Folklore: Welsh and Manx - John Rhys

Some Scottish Resources:
- The Gaelic Otherworld – John Gregorson Campbell, edited by Ronald Black
- Carmina Gadelica - Alexander Carmicheal
- The Silver Bough - F. Marian MacNeil

Some Gaulish Sources:
- The Celtic Gauls: Gods, Rites and Sanctuaries - Jean-Louis Brunaux
- Lady With A Mead Cup - Michael Enright

Some Manx Sources:
- Manx Calendar Customs - Cyril I. Paton
- Celtic Folklore: Welsh and Manx - John Rhys

Before You Go On

If you have made it all the way from the Bard course, the Ovate course and the past few chapters then you are VERY serious about your chosen path.

The heart of Druidry and the heart of most people who follow the Celtic religion lay in household practices and practices of groups they belong to. Things like honor, offering hospitality and forming a relationship with one's patron deities, spirits and ancestors as well as the Gods of the groups you may belong to. Remember you may join a group that honors the gods Lugh and Rosmerta while you honor Lugh and Brigit, there is nothing wrong with that, as the first set are the Gods of the tribe or tuatha you belong too and the second set are your household deities, this is something that we know the ancient Celts also did.

Before we go on, a word from someone who has been on the path a long time. Don't fall into the trap of being weekend pagans or quarterly ones who follow their path when they have the "time" for it or when they do a ritual or have something to ask of the gods. Druidry and the Celtic Religion are a way of life. We will be developing daily practices; they could be something as simple as saying a small prayer every morning or an offering ritual done everyday. We will also develop our yearly rituals and we will discuss the more controversial subject of Celtic shamanism. We will also be discussing seer- ship and divination. And finally, don't let anyone scare you off words like "worship", after all the Celtic religion is a RELIGION! I've noticed that most pagans seem to want to run away from words like that as they feel it is too close to what people following the monotheistic religions do. Not exactly, the word worship is a very innocent word. So let us take a look at it.

Definition of Worship:
Etymologically worship comes from Middle English "Worshipe", which means worthiness, respect, reverence paid to a divine being. It also goes back to Old English "Weorthscipe", which also means worthiness, respect, from "Weorth" that means worth and "Scipe" that means ship.

Worship means reverence offered to a divine being or supernatural power; also: an act of expressing such reverence. The key words here are respect, worthiness, reverence. Surely the Gods, land spirits and ancestors are worthy of such things? There is nothing humiliating or oppressing about it. So call it showing respect, or reverence or honoring but also don't be afraid of calling it worship. I promise there is nothing wrong with that.[1]

Before we go on please be sure you know which path you want to follow for the duration of this course. After you graduate it is totally up to you if you want to mix paths.

Endnotes

1 "worship." Merriam-Webster Online Dictionary. 2010. Merriam-Webster Online. 12 March 2010 http://www.merriam-webster.com/dictionary/worship

CHAPTER FIVE

Deities, Ancestors and Spirits Of The Land

The first step to developing personal practices is figuring out whom it is you want to honor/worship/revere/respect. (From now on these words are interchangeable)

In the Celtic culture the number 'three' figures largely in folklore and mythology. Now triads are also very famous, triads are a group of three things. One important triad will be where we will start the personal practices, the triad of the deities, ancestors and spirits of the land.

Let us start with the part of the triad that raises the most questions on the minds of people who follow the Celtic religion. I've had a lot of people ask me whether it was important to be of Celtic decent to be able to follow the Celtic religion. And who are these ancestors exactly, what if I am adopted and I don't know (or want to find out) who my ancestors are? Here is my answer (and other groups may have other answers), when I talk about ancestors I may be understood in three ways. They can be ancestors in DNA (you come from one of the Celtic countries) or they can be SPIRITUAL ancestors or ancestors of the heart (you've decided an interest in one of the Celtic countries and find yourself drawn to them (it)). Or they can be people you may have met and meant something to you or had an influence on your life and have now passed on (including your own physical ancestors known and unknown even if they are not Celtic).

The second part of the triad that is confusing is the spirits of the land. The ancient Celts honored various spirits of the land, of rocks, wells, trees, and holy wells. The honored the Aois Sí (the sidhe), otherwise known as the fairies or good folk. These spirits should be approached carefully, some are happy to give you the time while others don't want you near them. Always be careful how you approach them and how you act around them. Be sure never to "force" them into interacting with you and never use iron or steel around them. Some trees require a certain way of approaching them and the same goes for rocks or wells. These things are old Irish and Scottish traditions, which are still observed today. So how does this apply to living in a land that is not Celtic? You need to find out the spirits of the land YOU live in and incorporate that into your practice. Later in your assignment for this chapter you will know how to do this.

Now let us talk about the most important part of this triad and that is the deities. These are the gods and goddesses of the Celts. They fall into different categories: Patron deities or what I call household deities, and the deities of the tribe or group you maybe a part of. One of the main areas in the Celtic religion is to build a relationship with these deities and this relationship will lead to blessings and prosperity.

Since this is a class to develop personal practices we are going to look at the household deities only. The idea of household deities is very simple. They are the deities worshipped by you and your family. You may have one or more than one. Usually the deities will chose you or you may chose them until you feel your calling to a different one. Also be aware that at different times of your life this may change, it is not wrong. In ancient times the household deities were associated with the craft of the household head. For example a smith would worship Goibnu and a healer would worship Airmed. In the Appendices there is a list of some of the Celtic Gods and Goddesses we know.

Next we will talk about how to set up a hearth or altar for the triad we discussed.

CHAPTER SIX
Setting Up Your Hearth or Shrine

For the ancient Celts the Gods were everywhere. They were in trees, rocks, wells, and deserts. Offerings were left on rocks, in riverbeds or thrown into wells.

Putting together a place for you to commune with the Gods and the spirits of the land is very important. This will be the place to make your offerings, meditate and offer prayers, and request blessings and protection. There are two ways to do this, you may have a hearth or an altar in your home or you can have an outside shrine on your property.

Shrines would be great for people who have large properties or live next to a forest or river or mountain. The entire land is sacred after all. Offerings can be left at the base of a tree or a pile of rocks. Or you can set up on your own shrine out on the land. Use your imagination.

Hearths or altars are of course indoors. Use a place in your home that is geared towards peace and quiet, it could be a prominent place in the home or a private one. If you have children let them know how important that place is and you can actually use it as a gathering place to sit around and tell your children stories about the Celts or read them some of the myths. It would make a great connecting time for the two of you.

So what do you put on your altar or hearth? That is up to you. Just make sure all three parts of the triad from the previous chapter are represented. Let me give you an example. I learned from my grandfather to have a hearth in my home. My hearth is in the middle of my home, and near a window from which I can see the sky. I have two portable altars side by side. Table clothes cover both tables; my mother made one of the tablecloths and I made the other. One of the altars has pictures that I had drawn of my household deities, The Morrigan and Lugh, offering dishes and cups, and candles. On the second table I have pictures of my ancestors, two dishes, one with sand from a special place in the desert of Kuwait where the energies were high, and another dish with sand from Ireland and also candles and an offering dish. To me the dishes with sand represent the spirits of the land. I made all the dishes myself from clay, they aren't perfect but they are something that I labored on so they are also a sort of offering to the land spirits and the Gods. The pictures too are a labor of love. You can of course buy statues of the deities or you could use other things to represent them that is all up to you.

CHAPTER SEVEN

Ritual and Ritual Components

Well, now that you have a hearth/altar or shrine and you know who your patron deities are or at least you have an interest in contacting a certain deity, what is the next step? The next step is to start cultivating your personal daily practices. For that you need to learn about ritual.

So what exactly is a ritual? The English word ritual comes from the Latin word ritualis, which means of ceremonies. Ritualis is derived from the Latin word ritus, which means rite or ceremony. Ritus itself can be traced to the Proto-Indo-European root (*ar-). The earliest known usage of the word ritual in English dates back to the sixteenth century CE.[1]

Just like myths and religion, ritual also has its slew of theories, and not surprisingly these theories come from the same people who gave us the theories of myth and religion. Rituals at first were not studied independently but rather as part of something else. They were studied as part of anthropology, religious studies, history, sociology and psychology. The approaches to ritual include functionalism, psychoanalysis, phenomenology, structuralism, culturalism, performance studies, and practice theories, as well as cognitive, ethological, and sociological methods.

Looking for the definition of ritual in the dictionary yields the following: Ritual (noun): 1. The established form of ceremony, specifically the order of words prescribed for a religious ceremony. 2. (a) ritual observance, specifically a system of rites. (b) A ceremonial act or action, and (c) an act or series of acts regularly repeated in a set of precise manner. Ritual (adjective): 1. Of or relating to rites or a ritual, 2. According to religious law, and 3. Done in accordance with social custom or normal protocol.[2]

Now that we have an idea of what a ritual is let us talk about the components of ritual. The first thing you should decide is where to have it. Will it be indoors or outdoors? If it is outdoors will you need to build a space? If so, what kind of materials will you need? Is the space clean enough to use or will you need to beautify it? If you are doing this indoors, where will it happen, do you have the space for it? What kind of preparations will the space need?

Next you will need to gather the objects you need for the ritual. Make a list so you don't forget anything and be sure you plan early so that you have time to get the things you need.

Depending on what kind of ritual you will be doing you will need to choose a time for your ritual. Some times the timing is set and you have a certain window of time to perform the ritual and sometimes time does not matter. Be sure you know what type your ritual is.

The next two components of ritual go hand in hand. Sound, language and action are the particulars of the ritual. You will need to decide ahead of time whether you will need music, or whether you are going to perform a dance or whether it will be mostly through gestures and prayers.

Almost all rituals go through these steps, and if you go through these steps you will have a well- organized ritual.[3]

For the next chapter we will talk about making offerings to your deity and establishing a daily routine.

Endnotes

1 "Ritual" 2008 Access date: March 14, 2010.
http://www.myetymology.com/english/ritual.html

2 "ritual" Merriam-Webster Online Dictionary 2010 Access date: March 14, 2010
http://www.merriam- webster.com/dictionary/ritual

3 Grimes, Ronald L. Beginnings in Ritual Studies (Revised Edition). (Columbia: South Carolina University Press 1995) pp. 26 - 38

CHAPTER EIGHT

Practice Exercise: Offerings

People develop relationships with their household deities in different ways. One of these ways is by offering hospitality and friendship through the simple act of making an offering. It doesn't have to be complex or a highly structured ritual, you can just place the offerings in bowls and then present them to the deities in the name of the "Land, Sea and Sky".

Deciding what offerings to make can be difficult. Certain deities prefer certain things and you can learn that in time. Some things that are generally safe to use are bread, meats, hazelnuts, salmon, honey ale and mead.

Be sure not to allow your offerings to spoil or go moldy on the shrine, as that is bad manners. Be sure to dispose of these offerings in a very respectful way to the environment.

A Suggested Format for Daily Offerings:

The fire from the waters is here.
The fire from the lands is here.
The fire from the skies is here.
From below, from about, from above,
Fire has come to my hearth.[1]

Light the candles on your hearth and raise the offering in the air and say:

"I present these offerings to _____ to _____ in the name of the land, of the sky and of the sea and as a symbol of my hospitality, friendship and loyalty. I ask that you accept them and grant me."[2]

Then place the offering on your hearth. Then say a prayer depending on when you are making your offerings. Some people also like to meditate afterwards.

Endnotes

1 Serith, Ceisiwr. A Book of Pagan Prayers. (San Francisco: Weiser Book, 2002) p. 114.

2 Adopted from my friend Miachdhain's offerings ritual <http://delawarevalleyceltic.org/>.

CHAPTER NINE

ḃow to Create a Ritual

Well, now that you have a hearth/altar or shrine and you know who your patron deities are, or at least you have an interest in contacting a certain deity, and have performed at least one daily, weekly or monthly offering informal ritual, what is the next step? The next step is to start thinking about formal rituals.

We've already learned about the components of ritual generally but how do we actually create one? The first thing that you need to think about is whether or not you want to cast a circle in your rituals and whether or not you want to use the three realms system or the four directions system. Druid groups have used both of these things so there is no right or wrong answer here.

We don't realize it, but our days are filled with rituals. Little things we do the same way each day without thinking. Ruled by habit and the prodding of our sub-conscious minds. Think about the dish you set your car keys in when you come home from work. Is it simply so you can find them in the morning, or is it a sub-conscious symbol that you're home? Your morning coffee, do you drink it simply for the taste? Or is it a tool you use to mentally prepare you for your day? The rush of caffeine the jump-start you need to face the morning commute and the first hours in the office?

When we begin to look at ritual regardless of whether it is a sacred ritual or a mundane moment in life, we slowly begin to realize that most rituals are composed of eight simple stages. Sometimes we may combine steps together. Occasionally we may exclude one or two altogether. More often than not, all eight of the steps are present in both our daily rituals and our ceremonial rites.

The eight steps are as follows: cleaning, set-up, intent, raising energy, applying energy, sealing energy, giving thanks, and grounding.

We can't begin to fully embrace something until we can understand it. That's one of the probable reasons why our spiritual ancestors sought out the solstices. They divided the solar year into portions that they could understand. It is much simpler to grasp the change of energy from the summer solstice to winter solstice, than it is when we have no point of reference.

Our lives are a lot like that. If you find yourself growing tired at a certain time of day, your mood regularly changing for reasons you don't understand, or another shift in consciousness taking place at regular intervals, stop and take a look at your world. Consider what is happening before, during and after each step. It's likely you will find transitions there that can be embraced ritualistically. By doing so, you can begin to understand why you respond in certain ways. And anything that you understand, you can fully embrace or change as you see it. By understanding the components of ritual, we can create new rituals, as we require them.

We are going to take each of the 8 parts of the ritual and break them down. Let's start with the first one.

Preparing Sacred Space and setting it up:
We don't just hold rituals in any old space. We first designate a special area called Sacred Space. This is your shrine outside or your altar inside. One thought to keep in mind. A ritual doesn't begin when you cast a circle (because some people don't), it starts when you first think about doing a ritual. The ritual has already begun as you take a bath (if you are going to) and set up your altar and things needed for your ritual. Sacred Space is usually created in two to three steps: physical cleaning; astral cleaning and erecting a Sacred Circle if you are going to erect one. We all know what physical cleaning is but what is astral cleaning? Astral cleaning is done to rid the space of negative energy and psychic "dirt". Astral cleaning can be achieved by sprinkling salt water or burning purifying incense or a smudge stick, and walking from east around the space and back to east again. After you are done preparing your space, if you are going to cast a circle this would be when you would do it.

Make a Statement of Intent:
As the name suggests this is where you would state your intent as to why you are performing this ritual.

Invite Ancestors, Deities, and Land Spirits:
This would be where you invite the ancestors, deities and land spirits to join you in your ritual.

Raising Energy and applying and sealing it:
This can be done through meditations, guided meditations, visualization, drumming, and chanting. This would also be the time to perform the ritual, like for celebrating a Sabbath or honoring someone.

Giving thanks to the ancestors, deities, and land spirits:
This would be where you would thank the ancestors, deities and land spirits for co-ming when invited and making your ritual stronger. After this would be when you would take down the circle if you cast one.

Grounding:
This would be when the feasting can take place or you could meditate again to center yourself after the ritual and to release excess energy.

To help you plan a ritual please check out Appendix III where you will find a Personal Ritual Creation Worksheet and Appendix IV for two different examples of rituals, one with the three realms and no circle casting and one with the four directions and circle casting.

Also for ideas on how to open and close a circle and on how to use the three realms as opposed to the four directions I recommend Ceisiwr Serith's A Book of Pagan Prayer.

Also you can find the paganized version of the Carmina Gaedelica here (Part 1):
http://www.witchessabbats.com/index.php?option=com_content&view=article&id=7&Itemid=22

And here (Part2):
http://www.witchessabbats.com/index.php?option=com_content&view=article&id=13&Itemid=23

In appendix I you will find a selection of hymns and invocations of the original Carmina Gaedelica, the complete one can be found here:
http://www.sacred-texts.com/neu/celt/cg.htm

Sources

Lipp, Deborah. The Elements of Ritual: Air, Fire, Water & Earth in the Wiccan Circle (New York: Llewellyn Publications, 2003)

CHAPTER TEN
The Celtic Calendar

"Time rather than space, and processes of change rather than states of energy, provide the framework for the eight-fold year." (Greer page 75) "The eightfold year took many centuries to develop, and didn't take its present shape until modern times." (Greer page 75) What most people do not realize was that the current eight-fold year only developed in the 1950s when two English druids decided to expand the old calendar with what it is today. According to the book The Druidry Handbook the two druids were Ross Nichols and Gerald Gardner who later founded Wicca. (Unfortunately I am not able to confirm this with another source so I am writing this as a possible theory as to how the four-station year turned into eight and how the influence of Wicca came in.)

"The ancient Celts did not write down their beliefs, so we must piece together from such written sources as we have, Roman, Anglo-Saxon, Norse, and early Christian, and from archaeology, mythology, folk customs and other traditions both oral and practical, what these beliefs may have been." (Day page 4)

What makes this chapter difficult is that the Celts were not one tribe with a unified set of beliefs, they were rather many tribes with many beliefs that were unique to them. Also, all the resources available, books and Internet sites, are all tainted with Wiccan and Neo-pagan beliefs that have infiltrated the history. Another problem that must be taken into account is that the Celts did not write about their beliefs as mentioned before so we have to sift through what other people had to say about them including their prejudices.

According to many sources the ancient Celts may have only celebrated the Quarter Day of Samhain, Imbolc, Beltane, and Lughnasadh, because they believed that was when the worlds of the mortals and immortals were linked. These Quarter Days fall 40 days after solstices or equinoxes. The four quarters of the Celtic Year were: Earrach (spring) spoken like ear akh, Foghara (harvest) spoken like foe ghara, Samhradh (summer) spoken like sa wrah and Geimhradh (winter) spoken like give rah. The terms winter and summer were also applied to the two traditional halves of the year from 31st October to 30th April (Geimhradh) and 30th April to 31st October (Samhradh).

All of the four Celtic religious festivals were connected to things that happened within the farming calendar and they involved agricultural or pastoral activities. The Gauls had a calendar called the Coligny Calendar, which was found in the centre of France in a place called... Coligny! This calendar gives us the only evidence that the four festivals of Imbolc, Beltane, Lughnasadh, and Samhain, which were known to be celebrated in Ireland, were also celebrated elsewhere in the Celtic World.

According to the Dictionary of Celtic Myth and Legend Imbolc was one of the four main Celtic festivals of insular tradition. The festival was celebrated on February 1st and is thought to have been connected with the lactation of ewes. The feast was linked with the Irish Goddess Brigit, mother goddess and protectress of women in childbirth.

Moving into the realm of folklore, Imbolc starts at dusk on January 31st. It is the end of the winter and the beginning of the spring. Women were honoured as the winter hag gave way to the spring maiden. "Sowing and planting were traditionally begun, and the first lambs born. Cockerels were sacrificed at Imbolc to encourage the sun to return and rise in altitude, which event cockerels greeted by crowing. It was a bad omen if a cock crowed unexpectedly." (Day page 200)

In Ireland it was believed that Brigit will visit households to bless them so a rush matt is left outside to make her welcome and an offering of bread and milk. In the highlands of Scotland all activities are geared towards getting the blessing of Brigit, which was important for fertility and safe birth. "Imbolc seems to present itself as having much less importance than Samhain. It didn't concern either the military class or the King and was perhaps a more intimate and local affair." (Markale page 166)

From the Dictionary of Celtic Myth and Legend, Beltane is the second of the four great Insular Celtic seasonal festivals. It is believed to be celebrated on May 1st. The word Beltane means bright fire or goodly fire. It is associated with the start of open pasturing and the welcoming of the heat of the sun that promoted the growth of livestock and crops. This festival is important because it is considered to be the other extreme of the Celtic calendar. It is said that the mythical invasion of Ireland took place at this time.

In Ireland Beltane is also known as Cétshamain. It is possible that it was associated with the god Belenus. According to Irish vernacular records two bonfires were set by the Druids to assist the heat of the Sun in returning. In folklore the father of the house has the duty to bless and protect his family, which he did by the lighting of a candle. A farmer might bleed his cattle for their health, tasting the blood and pouring the reminder on the earth. Historically, the chief assembly at Tara, the official centre of Ireland, took place at this time. "The flames that sprang forth on the pyre of the hill of Tara, lit by the king of Ireland under the protection of the Druids, were more than a symbol. In the cycle of days and seasons they were the proof that life could be born from death." (Markale page 167) In Manx, there are the same customs, plus they light fires and drive their cattle through them. They also would not give fire to anyone. In Scotland the fires also represent purification of plants, animals, and humans. This festival is known in Wales as Calan Mai, and in Germanic countries as Walpurgis Night, when the witches and magicians gather to celebrate.

On August 1st and the fortnight preceding and following it Lughnasadh, which is a harvest festival, is celebrated. This festival was named after the great Irish god Lugh who founded this celebration in honour of his foster mother, Tailtiu. This festival is also an assembly on which political and legal matters were settled. A ritual to promote a successful harvest would have been preformed by Druids and other religious officials. At this time of year the King is supposed to be at the height of his power.

In Ireland this would be the ideal time for a hand- fasting. Traditionally this would be the day that Lugh defeated the corn bringer Com Dubh (spoken com doo) and won the corn for the Irish people but Christianity gave that honour to St. Patrick instead. On the Isle of Man there would be traditional visits to hilltops and sacred wells on this day. In the lowlands of Scotland it is called the festival of first fruits where bonfires are lit and handfastings happen. In the highlands of Scotland a procession around a sacred well on top of a hill top takes place.

The fourth major insular festival was Samhain. It is celebrated starting at dusk on October 31 and continues on to the day of November 1st. The word Samhain may have come from the Irish word samrad or the Gaulish word samon which refer to the warm season of the Celtic year. So Samhain signifies the end of the warm weather and the beginning of the winter. "A great assembly at Tara was held at this time, and the origin of the festival may have been linked with the rounding up and selection of domestic animals for winter culling, food provision or breeding." (Green page 36) Samhain was considered a dangerous time, as it is said that at this time the thin line between time and space is suspended and the spirits of the Otherworld are free to mingle with this one. The Druids are very much connected to Samhain as they are needed to control the spiritual energies of the day. Of course Samhain is considered the New Year.

In Ireland all the fires were extinguished to be relit again by the Druids. "In Irish homes, holy cakes were eaten. Black sheep were sacrificed. Animals were slaughtered for winter, a practice which was also carried out by the Anglo-Saxons." (Day page 346) The Irish would leave the entrances to burials open and kept the Interior lit and the cocks crowed inside so the dead can find their way. In the Isle of Man it was believed to be a dangerous time and even the windows in the animal houses or barns were sealed shut to keep the bad spirits away. There are similar traditions in Scotland.

This ends the Festivals that were celebrated in the time of the Druids. The next part will be the festivals added by later pagans and some of the folklore surrounding them. As mentioned before these celebrations were added in the 1900s. There have been different names given to the 4 remaining feasts. Some call them Litha, Ostara, Mabon and Yule; others call them Alban Herium (Litha), Alban Eiler (Ostara), Alban Elued (Mabon), and Alban Arthuan (Yule). The names of Alban are used in some Druidic orders that connect Druids to the Arthurian legends and the Masons. I shall use the pagan names given to the four remaining feasts.

Researching Yule it came to my attention that it was the winter solstice as celebrated by the Germanic tribes, and was later adopted by pagans. This celebration takes place on December 21st. This time is associated with death and rebirth of the Sun.

"According to Druidic mythology, the sun was wounded at noon today (December 21), dying slowly until death at sunset. It fell into the sea beyond the horizon, to be reborn in the morning." Of course the Coligny Calendar did not mention this festival.

Some of the folklore associated with this festival is that it lasted for 12 days and people would dress up animals like bulls and horses. This was more associated with Wales then anywhere else. There were mirror festivals in some parts of Ireland, Macca, Gaul, and Epona. There are some stone structures in Ireland like Newgrange, in county Meath, which are oriented to the winter solstice, so even though they might not have celebrated the winter solstice the Kings of Tara are said to be buried there so perhaps it had the symbolism that the King (sun) is dead but will be reborn in the Otherworld???

Next comes Ostara, this celebration takes place on March 21st, which falls on the Vernal or spring Equinox. In this festival the increasing power of the Sun is celebrated, this is done so that the animal offspring and the young plants will be healthy. Again this festival was not mentioned on the Coligny Calendar and so we know it was not celebrated by all the Celts. Loughcrew in County Meath, Ireland marks the Sunrise on this day with its Cairn T, which is also calibrated to the autumn equinox.

Litha, which is celebrated on June 21, is the Summer Solstice. "Litha celebrates the height of the sun's power and the abundance of summer. Nature is alive, and fields and fruits are growing towards harvest, but the blessing is mixed, for once light reaches its apogee it can only decline. Litha is a fairly modern term for the summer Solstice, and it may be derived from an Anglo-Saxon word for "moon" that referred to the sixth and seventh months of the year." (www.byzant.com)

Finally, the last festival celebrated by pagans and druids today is Mabon, which falls on September 21/22. "Mabon is the solar festival that marks the transition from the light to the dark half of the year: day and night are of equal length. On this day, the sun rises due east and sets due west. The autumn quarter of the year runs from Lughnasadh to Samhain, so Mabon marks the mid-point of autumn. By Mabon, the land is showing clear signs of the journey towards winter - leaves are beginning to turn and birds are gathering for migration. In Celtic mythology, Mabon was the Young God, abducted and imprisoned, only to return at a later date. This is thus an appropriate title for the day on which darkness gains the upper hand over light until the following equinox, Ostara. Mabon is the point at which, conceptually at least, the sun enters the sign of Libra, the Scales or Balance - the most appropriate sign for this day of perfect balance between darkness and light." (www.byzant.com)

It can be seen from the four main festivals that are known to have been from the Druids time, and the other four festivals added later, that the festivals were related to the farming year. So what good are they to the person who lives and works in the industrial world? The answer is very simple, the festivals when celebrated by the industrial pagan or Druid brings them closer to the nature, and tunes them into it. This brings them closer to what nature might need back from them. If they are in tune with it they may know how to help fix it and also be its voice.

Another reason that these festivals are important is that these festivals were not really meant to be preformed alone. If the history of all the festivals are looked at, it will be noticed that EVERYONE is expected to join in with no exceptions, and this is where the role of the Bards, Seers and Druids come in. The Druids might for example plan and lead, the Bards might tell the stories of old and recount history and the Seers might want to join in and perform divinations and tell of what they "see" past and future.

Some people who follow Druidry or Celtic polytheism also perform moon rites; some do it at the new moon while others do it at the full moon. This should be up to the organization, group or individuals. The evidence for the moon rites comes from mostly folklore as prayers can be found in the Carmina Gaedilica that indicate at least that there was some observance of this.

Sources

http://www.byzant.com/Mystical/Calendar/EightFestivals.aspx

http://www.hermetics.org/pdf/8SabbatsofWitchcraft.pdf

http://www.geocities.com/aryana_tisarana/index3.html

Greer, John Michael. The Druidry Handbook. Boston: Red Wheel/Weiser,LLC. 2006

Day, Brian. The Celtic Calendar. United Kingdom: C. W. Daniel Company Limited. 2003

Markale, Jean. The Druids: Celtic Priests of Nature. Vermont: Inner Traditions International. 1999

Green, Miranda Jane. Celtic Myths. Texas: University of Texas Press, 1998.

Green, Miranda J. Dictionary of Celtic Myth and Legend. New York: Thames & Hudson Ltd, 1997.

Green, Miranda J. The World Of The Druids. New York: Thames & Hudson Ltd, 1997.

CHAPTER ELEVEN

Celtic Shamanism

Celtic Shamanism has been a very controversial subject for many years. This is mainly due to the fact that the word shamanism is a term that comes from a Siberian tribal word for its spiritual practitioners: "shaman" (pronounced SHAH-mahn). So naturally people felt inclined to point out that just because we put the word Celtic in front of it does not make it an authentic Celtic practice. And yet let us take a closer look at the word Shamanism and how it is defined today.

Shamanism is an anthropological term referencing a range of beliefs and practices regarding communication with the spiritual world. Shamans perform a variety of functions depending on which culture they come from: healing; preserving the tradition by storytelling and songs; acting as a psychopomp (literal meaning, "guide of souls"). In some cultures, a shaman may fulfill several functions in one person.

The functions of a shaman may include either guiding to their proper abode the souls of the dead (which may be guided either one-at-a-time or in a cumulative group, depending on culture), and/or curing (healing) of ailments. The ailments may be either purely physical afflictions—such as disease, which may be cured by gifting, flattering, threatening, or wrestling the disease- spirit (sometimes trying all these, sequentially), and which may be completed by displaying some supposedly extracted token of the disease-spirit or else mental (including psychosomatic) afflictions—such as persistent terror (on account of some frightening experience), which may be likewise cured by similar methods. Usually in most languages a different term, other than the one translated "shaman", is applied to a religious official leading sacrificial rites ("priest"), or to a raconteur ("sage") of traditional lore; there may be more of an overlap in functions (with that of a shaman), however, in the case of an interpreter of omens or of dreams.[1]

To quote Mircea Eliade who spent a lot of time studying shamanism: "A first definition of this complex phenomenon, and perhaps the least hazardous, will be: shamanism = technique of ecstasy."[2] Ecstasy is a trance or trance-like state in which an individual transcends normal consciousness.

Now here is the thing. The word shaman was not applied by the Celts to their spiritual practitioners. They had different ones like File (pronounced feelyee), which is Irish Gaelic for "vision poet" or taibhsear (pronounced tah-shar), which is Scots Gaelic for "Vision Seer" or awenydd (pronounced ah-wen-ith), which is Welsh for "inspired one".

Shamanism exists among people who have animistic worldviews. Some cultures consider it spirituality but it can also exist separately from religion. Shamanism is a way of seeing the nature of the universe in a way that includes the invisible world of Spirits. This world is where the spirits of the land and the animals, deceased ancestors, the Gods and Goddesses, and the other spiritual entities live.

Shamans use altered consciousness so that they can send their spirits or souls into the spirit world to have direct experiences with particular spirits who become their friends, guides, guardians, instructors, and allies. The reason shamans seek this contact with the spirit world is to gain knowledge, wisdom, practical healing methods, and other vital information for the shaman's personal benefit or the community which he serves.

The spiritual practice of shamanism has some basic tenants:
• Shamanic journey.
• Ritual activities that honour the spirits of nature, the elements, animals, plants, seasons, and the deceased.
• Developing an art practice, a body practice, an academic practice, and a daily life practice, and keeping a journal.[3]

A shaman can be distinguished from mystics and visionaries by the *intentional* journey – called a shamanic journey or soul flight – into the spirit world. Basically, the shaman INITIATES contact by going directly into the spirit world. A Shamanic Journey is a combination of intentional and non-intentional experiences and sensations.

The Celtic Shaman's cosmos, like that of other Shamanic universal views, consists of three 'worlds'; the Lower world, the Upper world, and the Middle world (where we live in ordinary reality). What differentiates the Celtic Shaman's universal view from that of other Shamanic traditions is that these worlds are all connected by the great tree of life. Rooted in the Lower realm, its trunk extends upwards, through the Middle world and into the Upper world, where its branches hold the stars, the sun and the moon.

The Celtic Shaman travels the realms by climbing the tree (also seen as a great ladder or pole) into the Upper world. This is the realm of stars, celestial beings, and is the dwelling place of many Gods and spirits of the air.

The Lower world can be reached by descending the roots of the massive tree into the realm of the spirits of the earth and fire. Here the Celtic Shaman can meet with helper power animals and spirit guides. The Shaman sends his/her spirit (or consciousness) through a personal entrance into the Otherworld. Entries into the Otherworld are of two types, portals that "open into the Earth" for lower-world journeys and portals that "lead to the other side of the sky" for upperworld journeys.

Examples of lower-world openings or portals are through the roots of trees, through a spring or well or any other body of water, and through caves and tunnels. The upper-world journey openings or portals are through the stars which are believed to be holes that take you to the other side of the stars. Examples of how to get there include rainbows, sunbeams, sunrises, climbing up through trees and vines, through smoke from fires, or a cord that goes up to the sky.

Once you chose whatever method is more comfortable with you, you may start your shamanic journey. Right behind these openings you will find a tunnel, which will take you to the Otherworld. Spend the first few journeys exploring the opening and the tunnel and then venture into the Otherworld.[4]

Shapeshifting is an integral part of the Celtic Shamanic experience. The great Amergin had to commune and fuse his consciousness with the totality of Ireland in order to help the Milesians to conquer it.

I am the wind that blows across the sea;
I am a wave of the deep;
I am the roar of the ocean;
I am the stag of seven battles;
I am a hawk on the cliff;
I am a ray of sunlight;
I am the greenest of plants;
I am a wild boar;
I am a salmon in the river;
I am a lake on the plain;
I am the word of knowledge;
I am the point of a spear;
I am the lure beyond the ends of the earth;
I can shift my shape like a god.
- from the Song of Amergin

The ability to be simultaneously a part of many realities and existences is at the heart of the shamanic experience. The Celtic shaman deliberately seeks to take on the shape of another animal or being in order to call upon the power within the entity for healing or instruction. The ability of the shaman to send his or her own consciousness into the consciousness of another being and then return to one's own self is integral to the shaman's journey.

The Welsh bard Taliesin, often said to be the father of Celtic shamanism, also alluded to shapeshifting when he claimed:

I have been in many shapes:
I have been a narrow blade of a sword;
I have been a drop in the air;
I have been a shining star;
I have been a word in a book;
I have been an eagle;
I have been a boat on the sea;

I have been a string on a harp;
I have been enchanted for a year in the foam of water.
There is nothing in which I have not been.
- Taliesin

Taliesin was also known to have transformed himself into many other forms and guises in his attempt to escape the Goddess Ceridwen after imbibing of the brew of inspiration and wisdom.

In shamanic traditions, all people are guarded and watched over by a totem animal, which joins them at the time of their birth. In addition to this totem animal, which can remain with a person throughout their life, the shamanic practitioner acquires additional power animals at different times. These animal spirits serve as guides and spirit helpers. They may come of their own bidding, or may be called specifically because of their innate skills. In some cases the shaman draws upon the strength, the speed or the intuition of a particular animal, or the sharpness of the animals senses. In other situations the animal may tell the shaman things which the shaman cannot see for him- or herself.[5]

Throughout history animals have played important roles, both physically and psychically, providing material support and spiritual insight for human life.

Animals live naturally and spontaneously, doing what they are created to do without the self-doubt, uncertainty, and guilt that characterize human activity. Animals never lose their sense of themselves as spirit, responding with a fullness of spirit to whatever life presents to them, be it food, playful fun, sex, or death. Animals collectively possess greater strengths and powers. Ancient people saw animals as deities, of forms of deity, possessing wisdom, knowledge and an intuitive relationship with other life that humans have to struggle hard to acquire, if they can acquire it at all.

The ancestors looked to animal spirits as teachers, companions, and guides through the mysteries of life. The word "Power" in Power Animals refers to spiritual power that comes from inherent knowledge, information, or wisdom that the power animal willingly shares with its human companion.

Ways to meet Power Animals:
- Vision questing for a Power Animal.
- Dreaming for a Power Animal.
- Rattling or Drumming for a Power Animal.
- Dancing for a Power Animal.
- Journeying for a Power Animal.

Endnotes

1 "Shamanism" Wikipedia.org. 22 April 2010. Access Date: 24 April 2010
http://en.wikipedia.org/wiki/Shamanism

2 Eliade, Mircea. Shamanism: Archaic Techniques of Ecstasy. Princeton University
Press, USA. 1964.

3 Matthews, Caitlín and John. The Encyclopedia of Celtic Wisdom: A Celtic
Shaman's Sourcebook. Element Books Limited, Britain. 1994

4 Cowan, Tom. Shamanism: As a Spiritual Practice For Everyday Life. Crossing
Press, California. 1996

5 Matthews, Caitlín and John. The Encyclopedia of Celtic Wisdom: A Celtic
Shaman's Sourcebook. Element Books Limited, Britain. 1994

CHAPTER TWELVE

Divination

The Art of Divination is the method by which you try to find out about the past, present or future. There are hundreds of methods of divination, from the common to the curious to the bizarre. Many methods have been lost or obscured by the passing of time and the changing of civilizations. Some methods such as Astrology, Tarot Card reading, Tea Leave reading, Numerology, Runes, and Horoscopes have survived into the present and are both popular and in widespread use.

The diviner's job can entail many things: to find the source or cause of a problem; to serve as go-betweens for humans and spirits; to determine whether a person is suffering from a common illness or one caused by an upset ancestor; or to find the cause for a person's misfortune.

So if we look in the dictionary for the word "Divination" this is what we will find: The art or act of foretelling future events or revealing occult knowledge by means of augury or an alleged supernatural agency, an inspired guess or presentiment, something that has been divined.

Divination, like religion is universal and indigenous in one form or another. Some nations cultivated it to a higher degree than others, and their influence caused certain modes of divination to spread. Before Christianity, divination was practiced everywhere according to rites native and foreign. In early days, the priest and diviner were one person. When the Christian Church gained political power, it made all forms of divination capital crimes.

The eighth century A.D. saw the development of astrology and astronomy reach its peak, and is referred to as the 'Golden Age' because every field of learning such as Dharma, Astrological Science and Medicine enjoyed its highest patronage and development.

In France and Germany astrologers met even more encouragement than they received in England. Louis XI, a most superstitious man, entertained great numbers of them at his court; and Catherine de Medici, a most superstitious woman, hardly ever took any affair of importance without consulting them. She chiefly favoured her own countrymen. During the time she governed France, Italian conjurors, necromancers, and fortune-tellers of every kind overran the land. But the chief astrologer of that day, beyond all doubt, was the celebrated Nostradamus, physician to her husband, King Henry II.

The prophecies of Nostradamus consist of upwards of a thousand stanzas, each of four lines. They take such great latitude, both as to time and space, that they are almost sure to be fulfilled somewhere or other in the course of a few centuries.

But what about divination among the Celts, what do we know about that? The truth is we don't know much. And what we do know comes down to us from the Classical writers and they are biased against the Celts. Classical writers speak of the Celts as of all nations the most devoted to, and the most experienced in, the science of divination. Divination with a human victim is described by Diodorus. Libations were poured over him, and he was then slain, auguries being drawn from the method of his fall, the movements of his limbs, and the flowing of his blood.

Divination with the entrails was used in Galatia, Gaul, and Britain. Beasts and birds also provided omens. The course taken by a hare let loose gave an omen of success to the Britons, and in Ireland divination was used with a sacrificial animal. Among birds the crow was pre-eminent, and two crows are represented speaking into the ears of a man on a bas-relief at Compiegne. The Celts believed that the crow had shown where towns should be founded, or had furnished a remedy against poison, and it was also an arbiter of disputes. Birds were believed to have guided the migrating Celts, and their flight furnished auguries, because, as Deiotaurus gravely said, birds never lie. Divination by the voices of birds is believed to have been used by the Irish Druids. Omens were drawn from the direction of the smoke and flames of sacred fires and from the condition of the clouds.

The Imbas Forosnai, "illumination between the hands," was used by the File to discover hidden things. He chewed a piece of raw flesh and placed it as an offering to the images of the gods whom he desired to help him. If enlightenment did not come by the next day, he pronounced incantations on his palms, which he then placed on his cheeks before falling asleep. The revelation followed in a dream, or sometimes after awaking. Perhaps the animal whose flesh was eaten was a sacred one.

Another method was that of the Teinm Laegha. The File made a verse and repeated it over some person or thing regarding which he sought information, or he placed his staff on the person's body and so obtained what he sought. The rite was also preceded by sacrifice; this is why it is said that Saint Patrick prohibited both it and the Imbas Forosnai. Divination by dreams is also said to have been used by the continental Celts.[1]

The taghairm of the Highlanders was a survival from pagan times. The seer was usually bound in a cow's hide—the animal, it may be conjectured, having been sacrificed in earlier times. He was left in a desolate place, and while he slept spirits were supposed to inspire his dreams. Both among the continental and Irish Celts those who sought hidden knowledge slept on graves, hoping to be inspired by the spirits of the dead.[2]

Ogams were also engraved on rods of yews, and from these Druids divined hidden things. The method used may have been that of drawing one of the rods by lot and then divining from the marks upon it. The knowledge of astronomy ascribed by Caesar to the Druids were probably of a simple kind, and much mixed with astrology, and though it furnished the data for computing a simple calendar, its use was largely magical. This is one of the more modern of the Celtic divination methods. Appendix V has a list of the Ogams and translations of them, thanks to www.huntedwoodcrafts.com.

Another modern method of divination is Runes. Although it is more connected to the Norse than the Celts, modern Celtic practitioners still use it. Runes are an ancient Germanic alphabet, used for writing, divination and magic. They were used throughout northern Europe, Scandinavia, the British Isles, and Iceland from about 100 B.C.E. to 1600 C.E. Runic inscriptions of great age have even been found in North America, supporting stories that the Vikings arrived in the Americas long before Columbus. Runes are an oracle from which one seeks advice. They work best if you detail your current circumstances and then ask a specific question. Rune readings are sometimes obscure. They hint toward answers, but you have to figure out the details. This is when the rune casters intuition becomes paramount. Runic divination or "rune casting" is not "fortunetelling" in the sense that one actually sees the future. Instead, runes give one a means of analyzing the path that one is on and a likely outcome. The future is not fixed. It changes with everything one does.[3]

Although in some places the Runes numbered as many as 36 or as few as 16. Twenty-four of these were the basic Runes, or futhark. The name futhark comes from the first 6 Runes. There were 3 families of 8 Runes each, named after the Norse Gods Freyr, Hagal and Tyr. These three aettir, as they were called were:

- Freyr's Eight: Fehu, Uruz, Thurisaz, Ansuz, Raido, Kano, Gebo, Wunjo
- Hagal's Eight: Hagalaz, Nauthiz, Isa, Jera, Eihwaz, Perth, Algiz, Sowelu
- Tyr's Eight: Teiwaz, Berkana, Ehwaz, Mannaz, Laguz Inguz, Othila, Dagaz.[4]

For the meanings of the Runes please go to:
http://www.sunnyway.com/runes/meanings.html

Endnotes

1 Henderson, George. Survivals in Belief Among the Celts. The Macmillan Co., New York. 1911

2 MacCulloch, J. A. The Religion of the Ancient Celts. T. & T. Clark, Edinburgh. 1911

3 http://www.sunnyway.com/runes/

4 http://www.sacred-texts.com/pag/runes.txt

APPENDIX 1
Carmina Gadelica

Carmina Gadelica is an extensive work of hymns and incantations, published by Alexander Carmichael in 1900. It was originally written in both English and Scottish Gaelic. Below is a selection of the English translations hymns and incantations from the 1900 edition, without notes. They are overtly Christian in nature, but they can be adapted for use in pagan prayers and rituals (e.g. "God" can be supplanted with "the Gods" or the name of a specific God or Goddess).

RUNE BEFORE PRAYER

I AM bending my knee
In the eye of the Father who created me,
In the eye of the Son who purchased me,
In the eye of the Spirit who cleansed me,
    In friendship and affection.
Through Thine own Anointed One, O God,
Bestow upon us fullness in our need,
        Love towards God,
        The affection of God,
        The smile of God,
        The wisdom of God,
        The grace of God,
        The fear of God,
        And the will of God
To do on the world of the Three,
As angels and saints
Do in heaven;
    Each shade and light,
    Each day and night,
    Each time in kindness,
    Give Thou us Thy Spirit.

A PRAYER

    O God,
In my deeds,
In my words,
In my wishes,
In my reason,

And in the fulfilling of my desires,
In my sleep,
In my dreams,
In my repose.
In my thoughts,
In my heart and soul always,
May the blessed Virgin Mary,
And the promised Branch of Glory dwell,
    Oh! in my heart and soul always,
    May the blessed Virgin Mary,
    And the fragrant Branch of Glory dwell.

RUNE OF THE 'MUTHAIRN'

THOU King of the moon,
Thou King of the sun,
Thou King of the planets,
Thou King of the stars,
Thou King of the globe,
Thou King of the sky,
Oh! lovely Thy countenance,
Thou beauteous Beam.

Two loops of silk
Down by thy limbs,
Smooth-skinned;
Yellow jewels
And a handful
Out of every stock of them.

BLESS, O CHIEF OF GENEROUS CHIEFS

BLESS, O Chief of generous chiefs,
Myself and everything anear me,
Bless me in all my actions,
Make Thou me safe for ever,
    Make Thou me safe for ever.

From every brownie and ban-shee,
From every evil wish and sorrow,
From every nymph and water-wraith,
From every fairy-mouse and grass-mouse,
    From every fairy-mouse and grass-mouse.

From every troll among the hills,
From every siren hard pressing me,
From every ghoul within the glens,
Oh! save me till the end of my day.
Oh! save me till the end of my day.

DESIRES

MAY I speak each day according to Thy justice,
Each day may I show Thy chastening, O God;
May I speak each day according to Thy wisdom,
Each day and night may I be at peace with Thee.

Each day may I count the causes of Thy mercy,
May I each day give heed to Thy laws;
Each day may I compose to Thee a song,
May I harp each day Thy praise, O God.

May I each day give love to Thee, Jesu,
Each night may I do the same;
Each day and night, dark and light,
May I laud Thy goodness to me, O God.

INVOCATION FOR JUSTICE

I WILL wash my face
In the nine rays of the sun,
As Mary washed her Son
In the rich fermented milk.

Love be in my countenance,
Benevolence in my mind,
Dew of honey in my tongue,
My breath as the incense.

Black is yonder town,
Black are those therein,
I am the white swan,
Queen above them.

I will travel in the name of God,
In likeness of deer, in likeness of horse,
In likeness of serpent, in likeness of king:
Stronger will it be with me than with all persons.

THE SOUL SHRINE

GOD, give charge to Thy blessed angels,
  To keep guard around this stead to-night,
A band sacred, strong, and steadfast,
  That will shield this soul-shrine from harm.

Safeguard Thou, God, this household to-night,
  Themselves and their means and their fame,
Deliver them from death, from distress, from harm,
  From the fruits of envy and of enmity.

Give Thou to us, O God of peace,
  Thankfulness despite our loss,
To obey Thy statutes here below,
  And to enjoy Thyself above.

THE DEDICATION

THANKS to Thee, God,
Who brought'st me from yesterday
To the beginning of to-day,
Everlasting joy
To earn for my soul
With good intent.
And for every gift of peace
Thou bestowest on me,
My thoughts, my words,
My deeds, my desires
I dedicate to Thee.
I supplicate Thee,
I beseech Thee,
To keep me from offence,
And to shield me to-night,
For the sake of Thy wounds
With Thine offering of grace.

HOUSE PROTECTING

GOD, bless the world and all that is therein.
God, bless my spouse and my children,
God, bless the eye that is in my head,
And bless, O God, the handling of my hand;
What time I rise in the morning early,
What time I lie down late in bed,
    Bless my rising in the morning early,
    And my lying down late in bed.

God, protect the house, and the household,
God, consecrate the children of the motherhood,
God, encompass the flocks and the young;
Be Thou after them and tending them,
What time the flocks ascend hill and wold,
What time I lie down to sleep,
    What time the flocks ascend hill and wold,
    What time I lie down in peace to sleep.

BLESSING OF HOUSE

GOD bless the house,
From site to stay,
From beam to wall,
From end to end,
From ridge to basement,
From balk to roof-tree,
From found to summit,
    Found and summit.

THE NEW MOON

IN name of the Holy Spirit of grace,
In name of the Father of the City of peace,
In name of Jesus who took death off us,
Oh! in name of the Three who shield us in every need,
If well thou hast found us to-night,
Seven times better mayest thou leave us without harm,
    Thou bright white Moon of the seasons,
    Bright white Moon of the seasons.

HEY THE GIFT, HO THE GIFT

HEY the Gift, ho the Gift,
    Hey the Gift, on the living.

Son of the dawn, Son of the clouds,
Son of the planet, Son of the star,
    Hey the Gift, ho the Gift,
    Hey the Gift, on the living.

Son of the rain, Son of the dew,
Son of the welkin, Son of the sky,
    Hey the Gift, ho the Gift,
    Hey the Gift, on the living.

Son of the flame, Son of the light,
Son of the sphere, Son of the globe,
    Hey the Gift, ho the Gift,
    Hey the Gift, on the living.

Son of the elements, Son of the heavens,
Son of the moon, Son of the sun,
    Hey the Gift, ho the Gift,
    Hey the Gift, on the living.

Son of Mary of the God-mind,
And the Son of God first of all news,
    Hey the Gift, ho the Gift,
    Hey the Gift, on the living.

THE GIFT OF POWER

I AM the Gift, I am the Poor,
I am the Man of this night.

I am the Son of God in the door,
On Monday seeking the gifts.

Noble is Bride the gentle fair on her knee,
Noble the King of glory on her breast.

Son of the moon, Son of the sung
Great Son of Mary of God-like mind.

A cross on each right shoulder,
I am in the door, open thou.

I see the hills, I see the strand,
I see angels heralding on high.

I see the dove shapely, benign,
Coming with kindness and friendship to us.

GENEALOGY OF BRIDE

THE genealogy of the holy maiden Bride,
Radiant flame of gold, noble foster-mother of Christ,
Bride the daughter of Dugall the brown,
Son of Aodh, son of Art, son of Conn,
Son of Crearar, son of Cis, son of Carina, son of Carruin.

Every day and every night
That I say the genealogy of Bride,
I shall not be killed, I shall not be harried,
I shall not be put in cell, I shall not be, wounded,
Neither shall Christ leave me in forgetfulness.

No fire, no sun, no moon shall burn me,
No lake, no water, nor sea shall drown me,
No arrow of fairy nor dart of fay shall wound me,
And I under the protection of my Holy Mary,
And my gentle foster-mother is my beloved Bride.

THE BELTANE BLESSING

Everything within my dwelling or in my possession,
All kine and crops, all flocks and corn,
From Hallow Eve to Beltane Eve,
With goodly progress and gentle blessing,
From sea to sea, and every river mouth,
    From wave to wave, and base of waterfall.

Be the Three Persons taking possession of all to me belonging,
Be the sure Trinity protecting me in truth;
Oh! satisfy my soul in the words of Paul,
And shield my loved ones beneath the wing of Thy glory,
    Shield my loved ones beneath the wing of Thy glory.

Bless everything and every one,
Of this little household by my side;
Place the cross of Christ on us with the power of love,
Till we see the land of joy,
   Till we see the land of joy,
What time the kine shall forsake the stalls,
What time the sheep shall forsake the folds,
What time the goats shall ascend to the mount of mist,
May the tending of the Triune follow them,
   May the tending of the Triune follow them.

Thou Being who didst create me at the beginning,
Listen and attend me as I bend the knee to Thee,
Morning and evening as is becoming in me,
In Thine own presence, O God of life,
   In Thine own presence, O God of life.

KINDLING THE FIRE

I WILL raise the hearth-fire
As Mary would.
The encirclement of Bride and of Mary
On the fire, and on the floor,
And on the household all.

Who are they on the bare floor?
John and Peter and Paul.
Who are they by my bed?
The lovely Bride and her Fosterling.
Who are those watching over my sleep?
The fair loving Mary and her Lamb.
Who is that anear me?
The King of the sun, He himself it is.
Who is that at the back of my head?
The Son of Life without beginning, without time.

SMOORING THE FIRE

THE sacred Three
To save,
To shield,
To surround
The hearth,
The house,
The household,
This eve,
This night,
Oh! this eve,
This night,
And every night,
Each single night.
         Amen.

REAPING BLESSING

GOD, bless Thou Thyself my reaping,
Each ridge, and plain, and field,
Each sickle curved, shapely, hard,
Each ear and handful in the sheaf,
    Each ear and handful in the sheaf.

Bless each maiden and youth,
Each woman and tender youngling,
Safeguard them beneath Thy shield of strength,
And guard them in the house of the saints,
    Guard them in the house of the saints.

Encompass each goat, sheep and lamb,
Each cow and horse, and store,
Surround Thou the Rocks and herds,
And tend them to a kindly fold,
    Tend them to a kindly fold.

For the sake of Michael head of hosts,
Of Mary fair-skinned branch of grace,
Of Bride smooth-white of ringleted locks,
Of Columba of the graves and tombs,
    Columba of the graves and tombs.

THE PROTECTION OF THE CATTLE

PASTURES smooth, long, and spreading,
Grassy meads aneath your feet,
The friendship of God the Son to bring you home
To the field of the fountains,
     Field of the fountains.

Closed be every pit to you,
Smoothed be every knoll to you,
Cosy every exposure to you,
Beside the cold mountains,
     Beside the cold mountains.

The care of Peter and of Paul,
The care of James and of John,
The care of Bride fair and of Mary Virgin,
To meet you and to tend you,
     Oh! the care of all the band
     To protect you and to strengthen you.

THE CONSECRATION OF THE CLOTH

WELL can I say my rune,
Descending with the glen;
     One rune,
     Two runes,
     Three runes,
     Four runes,
     Five runes,
     Six runes.
     Seven runes,
     Seven and a half runes,
     Seven and a half runes.

May the man of this clothing never be wounded,
May torn he never be;
What time he goes into battle or combat,
May the sanctuary shield of the Lord be his.
What time he goes into battle or combat,
May the sanctuary shield of the Lord be his.

This is not second clothing and it is not thigged,
Nor is it the right of sacristan or of priest.

Cresses green culled beneath a stone,
And given to a woman in secret.
The shank of the deer in the head of the herring,
And in the slender tail of the speckled salmon.

CHARM FOR ROSE

THOU rose deathly, deadly, swollen,
Leave the udder of the white-footed cow,
Leave the udder of the spotted cow,
Leave, leave that swelling,
    And betake thyself to other swelling.

Thou rose thrawn, obstinate,
Surly in the udder of the cow,
Leave thou the swelling and the udder,
Flee to the bottom of the stone.

I place the rose to the stone,
I place the stone to the earth,
I place milk in the udder,
I place substance in the kidney.

CHARM OF THE SPRAIN

BRIDE went out
In the morning early,
With a pair of horses;
One broke his leg,
With much ado,
That was apart,
She put bone to bone,
She put flesh to flesh,
She put sinew to sinew,
She put vein to vein;
As she healed that
May I heal this.

FATH-FITH

FATH fith
Will I make on thee,
By Mary of the augury,
By Bride of the corslet,
From sheep, from ram,
From goat, from buck,
From fox, from wolf,
From sow, from boar,
From dog, from cat,
From hipped-bear,
From wilderness-dog,
From watchful 'scan,'
From cow, from horse,
From bull, from heifer,
From daughter, from son,
From the birds of the air,
From the creeping things of the earth,
From the fishes of the sea,
From the imps of the storm.

CHARM OF THE LASTING LIFE

I PLACE the charm on thy body,
And on thy prosperity,
The charm of the God of life
For thy protection.

The charm that Bride of the kine
Put round the fair neck of Dornghil,
The charm that Mary put about her Son,
Between sole and throat,
Between pap and knee,
Between back and breast,
Between chest and sole,
Between eye and hair.

The host of Michael on thy side,
The shield of Michael on thy shoulder,
There is not between heaven and earth
That can overcome the King of grace.

No spear shall rive thee,
No sea shall drown thee,

No woman shall wile thee,
No man shall wound thee.

The mantle of Christ Himself about thee,
The shadow of Christ Himself above thee,
From the crown of thy head
To the soles of thy feet.

The charm of God is on thee now,
Thou shalt never know disgrace.

Thou shalt go forth in name of thy King,
Thou shalt come in in name of thy Chief,
To the God of life thou now belongest wholly,
And to all the Powers together.

I place this charm early on Monday,
In passage hard, brambly, thorny,
Go thou out and the charm about thy body,
And be not the least fear upon thee.

Thou shalt ascend the crest of the hill,
Protected thou shalt be behind thee,
Thou art the calm swan in battle,
Preserved thou shalt be amidst the slaughter,
Stand thou canst against five hundred,
And thine oppressors shall be seized.

    The charm of God about thee!
    The arm of God above thee!

ST. BRIDE'S CHARM

THE charm put by Bride the beneficent,
On her goats, on her sheep, on her kine,
On her horses, on her chargers, on her herds,
Early and late going home, and from home.

To keep them from rocks and ridges,
From the heels and the horns of one another
From the birds of the Red Rock,
And from Luath of the Feinne.

From the blue peregrine hawk of Creag Duilion,
From the brindled eagle of Ben-Ard,

From the swift hawk of Tordun,
From the surly raven of Bard's Creag.

From the fox of the wiles,
From the wolf of the Mam,
From the foul-smelling fumart,
And from the restless great-hipped bear.
*   *   *   *   *
*   *   *   *   *
From every hoofed of four feet,
And from every hatched of two wings.

THE CHARM OF THE FIGWORT

I WILL pluck the figwort,
With the fruitage of sea and land,
The plant of joy and gladness,
The plant of rich milk.

As the King of kings ordained,
To put milk in pap and gland,
As the Being of life ordained,
To place substance in udder and kidney,
With milk, with milkiness, with butter milk,
With produce, with whisked whey, with milk-product,
With speckled female calves,
Without male calves,
With progeny, with joy, with fruitage,
With love, with charity, with bounty,

Without man of evil wish,
Without woman of evil eye,
Without malice, without envy, without 'toirinn,'
Without hipped bear,
Without wilderness dog,
Without 'scan foirinn,'
Obtaining hold of the rich dainty
    Into which this shall go.
Figwort of bright lights,
Fruitage to place therein,
With fruit, with grace, with joyance.

THE FAIRY WORT

PLUCK will I the fairy wort,
With expectation from the fairy bower,
To overcome every oppression,
As long as it be fairy wort.

Fairy wort, fairy wort,
I envy the one who has thee,
There is nothing the sun encircles,
But is to her a sure victory.

Pluck will I mine honoured plant
Plucked by the great Mary, helpful Mother of the people,
To cast off' me every tale of scandal and flippancy,
Ill-life, ill-love, ill-luck,
Hatred, falsity, fraud and vexation,
Till I go in the cold grave beneath the sod.

THE YARROW

I WILL pluck the yarrow fair,
That more benign shall be my face,
That more warm shall be my lips,
That more chaste shall be my speech,
Be my speech the beams of the sun,
Be my lips the sap of the strawberry.

May I be an isle in the sea,
May I be a hill on the shore,
May I be a star in waning of the moon,
May I be a staff to the weak,
Wound can I every man,
Wound can no man me.

THE ASPEN

MALISON be on thee, O aspen tree!
  On thee was crucified the King of the mountains,
In whom were driven the nails without clench,
  And that driving crucifying was exceeding sore--
  That driving crucifying was exceeding sore.

Malison be on thee, O aspen hard!
  On thee was crucified the King of glory,
Sacrifice of Truth, Lamb without blemish,
  His blood in streams down pouring--
  His blood in streams down pouring.

Malison be on thee, O aspen cursed!
  On thee was crucified the King of kings,
And malison be on the eye that seeth thee,
  If it maledict thee not, thou aspen cursed--
  If it maledict thee not, thou aspen cursed!

SHAMROCK OF LUCK

THOU shamrock of good omens,
Beneath the bank growing
Whereon stood the gracious Mary,
    The Mother of God.

The seven joys are,
Without evil traces,
On thee, peerless one
Of the sunbeams--

    Joy of health,
    Joy of friends,
    Joy of kine,
    Joy of sheep,
    Joy of sons, and
    Daughters fair,
    Joy of peace,
    Joy of God!

The four leaves of the straight stem,
Of the straight stem from the root of the hundred rootlets,
Thou shamrock of promise on Mary's Day,
Bounty and blessing thou art at all times.

THE SHAMROCK OF POWER

THOU shamrock of foliage,
Thou shamrock of power,
Thou shamrock of foliage,
Which Mary had under the bank,
Thou shamrock of my love,
Of most beauteous hue,
I would choose thee in death,
To grow on my grave,
    I would choose thee in death,
    To grow on my grave.

GOD OF THE MOON

GOD of the moon, God of the sun,
God of the globe, God of the stars,
God of the waters, the land, and the skies,
Who ordained to us the King of promise.

It was Mary fair who went upon her knee,
It was the King of life who went upon her lap,
Darkness and tears were set behind,
And the star of guidance went up early.

Illumed the land, illumed the world,
Illumed doldrum and current,
Grief was laid and joy was raised,
Music was set up with harp and pedal-harp.

APPENDIX II
Listing of Some of the Celtic Gods and Goddesses

The Celtic Gods and Goddesses are numerous. There are a total of 400 names mentioned on artifacts or epiteths, with 300 names only mentioned once so as you can see, there is no way ALL the Gods can be listed here. I will do my best though! The list will be multi-parted because of space.

Gods and Goddesses starting with A:

Abandinus (British God): is an obscure Celtic deity, possibly a river-god. He is currently known only from a single inscription from Godmanchester in Cambridge-shire, England: a bronze votive feather is dedicated to him with the fragmentary text "to the god Abandinus, Vatiaucus gave this from his own resources" inscribed on a plaque.

Aonghus (Irish God): Aengus (Áengus, Óengus, Aonghus) aka Aengus Óg ("Aengus the Young"), Mac ind Óg ("son of the young"), Maccan or Mac Óg ("young son") is a member of the Tuatha Dé Danann and probably a god of love, youth and poetic inspiration. He was said to have four birds symbolizing kisses flying about his head (whence, it is believed, the xxxx's symbolizing kisses at the end of lovers' letters come from). His parents were the Dagda and Boann. He was said to have lived at Newgrange by the river Boyne.

Áine (Irish Goddess): (pronounced "awnya" (Connacht Irish) or "enya" (Ulster Irish) is a goddess of love, growth, and cattle, also associated with light and perhaps the sun. She is the daughter of Egobail, and sister of Aillen and/ or Fennen.

Airmed (Irish Goddess): was one of the Tuatha Dé Danann. With her father Dian Cecht and brother Miach, she healed those injured in the Second Battle of Magh Tuiredh. Because she collected and organized the herbs that grew from Miach's grave, she is particularly associated with herbalism. Along with Dian Cecht, Ocht-riullach, and Miach, she was one of the enchanters whose incantation sung over the well of Sláine was able to resurrect the dead.

Amaethon or **Amathaon** (Welsh God): (Welsh 'great ploughman'), was a son of Dôn and a presumed agricultural deity.

Antenociticus: appears at only one site in Britain, on Hadrian's Wall, where three altars to the god were found within the ruins of a small temple. This god is not mentioned on any known Roman altar stones from the continent, and is therefore thought to be a native British deity.

Arawn (Welsh God): was the Lord of the Underworld, which was called Annwn.

Arianrhod (Welsh Goddess): ("silver wheel") She is the daughter of Dôn and the sister of Gwydion and Gilfaethwy; the Welsh Triads give her father as Beli Mawr. In the Mabinogion her uncle Math ap Mathonwy is the King of Gwynedd, and during the course of the story she gives birth to two sons, Dylan Eil Ton and Lleu Llaw Gyffes, through magical means.

Arnemetia (British Goddess): was a water goddess worshipped in Britain. Her shrine was at Aquae Arnemetiae ("waters of Arnemetia"), modern Buxton in Derbyshire, England. Arnemetia's name contains the Celtic word "nemeton", meaning "sacred grove", so her name is interpreted as "she who dwells over against the sacred grove".

Artio (Gaulish Goddess): was a goddess of the bear, and was worshipped at Berne, which actually means "bear".

Abellio (also Abelio and Abelionni) (Gaulish God): He may have been a god of apple trees.

Abnoba (Gaulish goddess): who was worshipped in the Black Forest and surrounding areas. She has been interpreted to be a forest and river goddess, and is known from about nine epigraphic inscriptions.

Agrona was a goddess of strife and war worshipped in Britain.

Alaunus was a Gaulish god of the sun, healing and prophecy. A major branch of Celts called this God Fin.

Ambisagrus was a Gaulish god of thunder and lightning.

Ancamna (Gaulish goddess) was a water goddess worshipped particularly in the valley of the Moselle River.

Andarta was a warrior goddess worshipped in southern Gaul. Inscriptions to her have been found in Bern, Switzerland as well as in southern France. Like the similar goddess Artio, she was associated with the bear.

Andraste (British goddess): was a Celtic goddess thanked by Boudicca while fighting against the Roman occupation of Britain in AD 61. She is mentioned only once.

Avernus was the god of the Gallic Avernii.

Arduinna was the eponymous goddess of the Ardennes Forest (primarily in Belgium and Luxembourg). Her cult thus originated in the Ardennes, and the forest name from her. She was later assimilated to the Roman Diana.

Aufaniae was a collective name for a group of Celtic mother goddesses worshipped throughout Celtic Europe. They are known only from symbolical inscriptions and they appear to have been found mainly in the German Rhineland.

Aveta or Lyregwyn (Gaulish goddess): was a goddess of female-fertility, childbirth and midwives, also associated with all fresh water. Aveta is known mainly from clay figurines found at Toulon-sur-Allier, France. The models show the goddess with infants at the breast and apparently she is concerned with nursing mothers. The figure is often accompanied by a small lap-dog.

Gods and Goddesses starting with B:

Badb (Irish Goddess): was a goddess of war who took the form of a crow, and was thus sometimes known as Badb Catha (battle crow). She often caused confusion among soldiers to move the tide of battle to her favoured side. The Badb is associated with the beansidhe, and is said to have been crucial in the battle against the Fomorians. With her sisters Macha and the Morrígan, daughters of Ernmas, she was part of a trio of war goddesses called collectively the Morrígan.

Banba (Irish Goddess): daughter of Ernmas of the Tuatha Dé Danann, was one of the patron goddesses of Ireland. Her husband was Mac Cuill. With her sisters, Fodla and Ériu, she was part of an important triumvirate of goddesses.

Belatu-Cadros ("fair shining one" or "fair slayer"), also rendered Belatucadros or Belatucadrus, was a deity worshipped in northern Britain, particularly in Cumberland and Westmorland. He may be related to Belenus and Cernunnos, and was equated in the Roman period with Mars. He appears to have been worshipped by lower-ranked Roman soldiers as well as by Britons.

Belenus (also Belinus, Belenos, Belinos, Belinu, Bellinus, Belus, Bel) was a deity worshipped in Gaul, Britain and Celtic areas of Italy, Austria and northern Spain. He had shrines from Aquileia on the Adriatic to Inveresk in Scotland. His name means, "shining one" or "henbane god" and he is associated with heat and healing. He may be the same deity as Belatu-Cadros. In the Roman period he was identified with Apollo. His consort was Belisama.

Belisama (also Belesama) was a goddess worshipped in Gaul and Britain. She was connected with lakes and rivers, fire, crafts and light. Belisama was identified with

Minerva/ Athena and has been compared with Brigid. She was the consort of Belenus, with whom she shared certain attributes. Her name means "most brilliant".

Boann or **Boand** (Irish Goddess) was the goddess of the River Boyne. According to the Lebor Gabála Érenn she was the daughter of Delbáeth, son of Elada, of the Tuatha Dé Danann. Her husband is variously Nechtan, Elcmar or Nuada. Her lover is the Dagda, by whom she had her son, Aengus.

Bodb Derg (Irish God): was a son of Eochaid Garb or the Dagda, and the Dagda's successor as King of the Tuatha Dé Danann.

Borvo ("to boil"), also **Bormo**, **Bormanus** (Gaulish God): was a deity was associated with mineral springs, hot springs and healing.

Brigit or **Brighit** ("exalted one") was the daughter of the Dagda (and therefore one of the Tuatha Dé Danann) and wife of Bres of the Fomorians. She had two sisters, also named Brighid, and is considered a classic Celtic Triple Goddess. Brighid was associated with perpetual, sacred flames; Brighid was also connected to holy wells, at Kildare and many other sites in the Celtic lands.

Brigantia was a goddess who is attested several places in Britain and Europe. She was the tutelary goddess of the Brigantes in northern Britain (modern Yorkshire) and of the Brigantes on Lake Constance in Austria (modern Bregenz).

Buxenus was the god of box trees, worshipped primarily in Gaul alongside Abellio, Fagus and Robur.

Gods and Goddesses starting with C:

Cailleach also known as the Cailleach Bheur, is generally seen as a divine hag, a creator, and possibly an ancestral deity or deified ancestor. The word simply means 'old woman' in modern Scottish Gaelic, and has been applied to numerous mythological figures in both Scotland and Ireland. In Scotland, where she is also known as Beira, Queen of Winter, she is credited with making numerous mountains and large hills, which are said to have been formed when she was striding across the land and accidentally dropped rocks from her apron. In other cases she is said to have built the mountains intentionally, to serve as her stepping-stones. She carries a hammer for shaping the hills and valleys. In partnership with the goddess Brìghde, the Cailleach is seen as a seasonal deity or spirit, with The Cailleach Bheur ruling the winter months between Samhuinn and Bealltainn, and Brìghde ruling the summer months between Bealltainn and Samhuinn.

Camulus or **Camulos** was the god of war of the Remi, a Celtic tribe, who lived in the area of today's Belgium. Traces of his cult are also found in Britain.

Carldwen: Goddess of Corn and Protector of Poets.

Crom Cruach or **Cromm Crúaich**, also known as Cenn Cruach or Cenncroithi, was a deity of pre-Christian Ireland, reputedly propitiated with human sacrifice, whose worship is said to have been ended by St.Patrick.

Ceridwen was a magician, mother of Taliesin, Morfran, and a beautiful daughter Crearwy (or Creirwy). Her husband was Tegid Foel, and they lived near Bala Lake in Wales.

Cernunnos is a Celtic god whose representations were widespread in the ancient Celtic world. As a horned god, Cernunnos is associated with horned male animals, especially stags and the ram-headed snake; this and other attributes associate him with produce and fertility.

Cliodhna (Cliodne, Clídna, Cliona, Cleena) was a goddess of love and beauty, known as the queen of the Munster fairies. She was said to have three brightly coloured birds who ate apples from an otherworldly tree and whose sweet song healed the sick. She left the otherworldly island of Tir Tairngire ("the land of promise") to be with her mortal lover, Ciabhán, but drowned as she slept in Glandore harbour in County Cork: the tide there is known as Tonn Chlíodhna, "Cliodhna's Wave".

Clota was the patron goddess of the River Clyde. Perhaps worshiped by the local Welsh-speaking Damnonii tribe who held the territory, which later was to become the Kingdom of Strathclyde. The Damnonii allied themselves with Rome who recorded and mapped the Clota estuary. During the Antonine period the Romans built the Antonine Wall from the Forth to the Clyde and created a causeway stretching across the 'Clota', which linked the forts at Bishopton, Greenock and Largs, to the Antonine Wall.

Camma (Breton Goddess): was a hunting goddess

Cissonius (also Cisonius, Cesonius) was an ancient Gaulish god. He was probably a god of trade and protector of travelers.

Cocidius was a deity worshipped in northern Britain. The Romans equated him with Mars, god of war and hunting and with Sylvanus, god of forests, groves and wild fields. Like Belatu- Cadros, lower-ranked Roman soldiers as well as Britons probably worshipped him.

Condatis ("waters meet") was a deity worshipped primarily in northern Britain but also in Gaul. He was associated with the confluences of rivers, in particular the Tyne and the Tees. In Roman times he was equated with Mars, probably in his healing function.

Coventina was a Romano-British goddess of wells and springs.

Gods and Goddesses starting with D:

The Dagda is an important god of Irish mythology. He is the supreme god in Irish mythology. His name means "The Good God" (Old Irish deagh dia; Modern Irish dea-Dia), not necessarily good in a moral sense, but good at everything, or all-powerful. The Dagda is a father-figure (he is also known as Eochaid Ollathair, or Eochaid All-Father) and a protector of the tribe. In some texts his father is Elatha, in others his mother is Ethlinn. Irish tales depict the Dagda as a figure of immense power, armed with a magic club and associated with a cauldron. The club was supposed to be able to kill nine men with one blow; with the handle he could return the slain to life. The cauldron was bottomless, capable of feeding an army. He also possessed Daurdabla, a richly ornamented magic harp made of oak which, when the Dagda played it, put the seasons in their correct order; other accounts tell of it being used to command the order of battle. He possessed two pigs, one of which was always growing whilst the other was always roasting, and ever-laden fruit trees. He's the God of Life and Death, War, Banquets and Magic.

Danu or **Dana** was the mother goddess of the Tuatha Dé Danann (peoples of the goddess Danu). However, little is recorded about her as an individual. Some scholars believe Danu and Anu (also Ana) are the same deity, while others state that the two are separate individuals. Danu's Welsh equivalent is Dôn, Irish Goddess of Wind, Wisdom and Fertility.

Dian Cécht was a god of healing. He was the healer for the Tuatha Dé Danann and the father of Cian, Cú, and Cethen. His other children were Miach, Airmed, Étan the poetess, and Ochtriullach. He blessed a well called Slane so that the Tuatha Dé could bathe in when wounded; they became healed and continued fighting. It would heal any wound but decapitation.

Dôn was a Welsh mother goddess. She is the consort of Beli Mawr and the mother of Arianrhod, Gwydion, Gilfaethwy, Gofannon and Amaethon.

Donn, or the Dark One, is the Lord of the Dead and father of Diarmuid Ua Duibhne, whom he gave to Aengus Og to be nurtured. Donn is regarded as the father of the Irish race; a position similar to that of Dis Pater and the Gauls, as noted by Julius Caesar.

Dylan Ail Don is a sea-god in Welsh mythology, a son of Arianrhod and Gwydion. He is sometimes said to be a god of darkness.

Damara was a fertility goddess worshipped in Britain. She was associated with the month of May/Beltaine.

Damona was a goddess worshipped in Gaul as the consort of Apollo Borvo and of Apollo Moritasgus. Damona's name is interpreted as "Divine Cow" based on its resemblance to damos or "cow". She has sometimes been linked with the Irish goddess Boand on the basis of this bovine association.

Dea Matrona ("divine mother goddess") was the goddess of the river Marne in Gaul.

Dis Pater, or **Dispater**, was a Roman and Celtic god of the underworld, later subsumed by Pluto or Jupiter. Originally a chthonic god of riches, fertile agricultural land, and underground mineral wealth, he was later commonly equated with the Roman deities Pluto and Orcus, becoming an underworld deity. Dis Pater was commonly shortened to simply Dis. This name has since become an alternate name for the underworld or a part of the underworld.

Gods and Goddesses starting with E:

Epona was a protector of horses, donkeys, and mules. She was particularly a goddess of fertility, as shown by her attributes of a patera, cornucopia, and the presence of foals in some sculptures.

Ériu, daughter of Ernmas of the Tuatha Dé Danann, was the eponymous patron goddess of Ireland. Her husband was Mac Gréine ('Son of the Sun'). She was the mother of Bres by Prince Elatha of the Fomorians. The English name for Ireland comes from the name Ériu and the Old Norse or Anglo-Saxon word land. With her sisters, Banba and Fodla, she was part of an important triumvirate of goddesses.

Esus or **Hesus** ("lord" or "master") was a Gaulish god known from two monumental statues and a line in Lucan's Bellum civile. The two statues on which his name appears are the Pillar of the Boatmen from among the Parisii and a pillar from Trier among the Treveri. In both of these, Esus is portrayed cutting branches from trees with his axe. Esus is accompanied, on different panels of the Pillar of the Boatmen, by Tarvos Trigaranus (the 'bull with three cranes'), Jupiter, Vulcan, and other gods. The name Esus is a cognate of Zeus who as the tree-splitter is associated with both axes and trees, he is a war God.

Gods and Goddesses starting with F:

Fagus (Gaulish God) was a god of beech trees.

Fea: 'The Hateful' — another Warrior Goddess associated with the Morrigan.

Fótla was an Irish goddess, the sister of Banba and Eriu. The three sisters competed to have Amergin name Ireland after them.

Fuamach (Irish Goddess): Goddess of Malicious Jealousy.
Gods and Goddesses starting with G:

Grannus (also Gramnos, Gramnnos) was a god of healing and mineral springs. His cult was centered in Aquae Granni (now Aachen, Germany).

Gods and Goddesses starting with H:

Herne: See Cernunnos.

Hooded Spirits, or **Genii Cucullati** are figures found in religious sculpture across the Romano-Celtic region from Britain to Austria, depicted as "cloaked scurrying figures carved in an almost abstract manner". They are found with a particular concentration in the Rhineland. In Britain they tend to be found in a triple deity form, which seems to be specific to the British representations (De la Bedoyère). They may be fertility spirits of some kind.

Gods and Goddesses starting with I:

Icaunus was the god of the river Yonne in Gaul.

Icovellauna was a Celtic goddess worshipped in Gaul. Her places of worship included a temple in Metz, originally built over a spring; a cult centre in Malzéville, from which five inscriptions dedicated to her have been recovered; and Trier. All of these places lie in the valley of the Moselle or Meurthe rivers of eastern Gaul, in what are now Lorraine in France and Rhineland-Palatinate in Germany. Icovellauna is a "water-goddess" who "presided over the nymphaeum at Sablon in the Moselle Basin, a thermal spring-site".

Gods and Goddesses starting with L:

Loucetios was a Gaulish god invariably identified with Mars. About a dozen inscriptions in his honour have been recovered, mainly from eastern Gaul with a particular concentration among the Vangiones (a Rhenish tribe). Loucetios is often accompanied by Nemetona. Inscriptions to him have also been found at Bath and Angers. He has been interpreted to be a god of thunder. His name may be derived from the Proto-Indo-European root *leuk- ("white light").

Lugus was a Celtic deity attested in inscriptions in Gaul, Germany and Switzerland (RIG, G-159) and worshipped in Britain, in Ireland, and in other ancient Celtic regions. His cult in the Iberian Peninsula was centered among the Celtiberians. In the northwest, in Gallaecia, as Lugo he is mentioned in three inscriptions from

Sober and Otero del Rey. Archaeological inscriptions indicate that Lugus or Lugh was an important deity for the Astures and one of their most important tribes, the Luggones, was named after him. He may appear in the plural: Lucubo Arquienobo, Locoubu Arquienis. Garcia Quintela (2003) suggests that a sanctuary dedicated to this native god might have been the basis for the foundation of the city of Lucus Augusti, the modern Lugo, Galicia. An inscription from Peña Amaya, north of Burgos, that is dedicated to Dibus M(agnis?) Lucubo(s) testifies to the supreme nature of this god among Cantabrian people. Several Latin inscriptions containing dedications to the Lugoves, a plural form again, have been found in Switzerland and Spain). His importance in the Celtic pantheon can be deduced from a multitude of ancient place names and from figures in later Celtic mythology, such as the Irish Lugh and Welsh Lleu Llaw Gyffyes.

Luxovios, Latinized as Luxovius was the god of the waters of Luxeuil, worshipped in Gaul. He was a consort of Bricta. The thermal spring sanctuary at Lexeiul produced evidence of the worship of other deities, including the sky- horseman who bears a solar wheel, and Sirona, another deity associated with healing springs.

Gods and Goddesses starting with M:

Maponos or **Maponus** ("divine son") was a god of youth and love known mainly in northern Britain but also in Gaul. In Roman times he was equated with Apollo.

Macha is a goddess in Irish mythology linked with horses, battle, and sovereignty. She is said to have collected the heads of the slain, which were known as "Macha's acorn crop". Though possibly a triple goddess herself, she is often seen as one aspect of the Irish triple goddess of battle and sovereignty, the Morrígan.

Manannán mac Lir is the god of the sea. He is often seen as a psychopomp, and considered to have strong connections to the Otherworld islands of the dead, the weather, and the mists between the worlds. He is usually counted as one of the Tuatha Dé Danann, although most scholars consider him to be of an older race of deities.

Matunus or **Matunos** was a Bear god in Brythonic Celtic polytheism. His name may be derived from the same root as Proto-Celtic *matu- meaning bear. He was worshipped in Roman Britain and altar-stones raised to him have been recovered in the United Kingdom, such as at High Rochester and at Risingham.

The **Morrígan** ("terror" or "phantom queen") or, less accurately but still used in some texts, Mórrígan ("great queen"), (aka Morrígu, Morríghan, Mor-Ríoghain) is a figure from Irish mythology who appears to have once been a goddess, although she is not explicitly referred to as such in the texts. She is usually seen as a terrifying figure. She is associated with war and death on the battlefield, sometime appearing in the form of a carrion crow, premonitions of doom, and with cattle. She is often considered a war deity comparable with the Germanic Valkyries, although her association with cattle also suggests a role connected with fertility and the land. She is often interpreted as a triple goddess, although membership of the triad varies: the most common combination is the Morrígan, the Badb and Macha, but sometimes includes Nemain, Fea, Anann and others.

Gods and Goddesses starting with N:

Nantosuelta was a goddess of fire and fertility in Gaul.

Nechtan was the father and/or husband of Boann. He may be Nuada under another name, or his cult may have been replaced by that of Nuada. Only he and his three cup-bearers were permitted to visit the well of Segais, into which nine sacred hazel trees dropped their wisdom- bearing nuts. When Boann visited the well, it overflowed and chased her to the coast, forming the river Boyne. The God who owned the hill upon which stood the Holy Well of All Knowledge.

Nemetona ("shrine") was a goddess worshipped in eastern Gaul and Roman Britain. Her name suggests the common interpretation that she was a goddess of temples and sacred groves, protecting ancient Celtic ceremonial sites held outdoors in sacred groves of trees. She is believed to continuously watch over sacred sites, and is invoked today by some neo-pagan practitioners to help establish sacred spaces.

Nemain (or **Nemhain**) was a goddess of war, and possibly an aspect of the Morrígan. Her name means 'panic' or 'frenzy', and causing it among warriors was her specialty.

Nemausus is often said to have been the Celtic patron god of Nemausus (Nîmes). The god does not seem to exist independently of the locality. The city certainly derived its name from Nemausus, which was perhaps the sacred wood in which the Celtic tribe of the Volcae Arecomici (who of their own accord surrendered to the Romans in 121 BC) held their assemblies, or was perhaps the local Celtic spirit guardian of the spring that originally provided all water for the settlement, as many modern sources suggest.

Nodens (**Nudens**, **Nodons**) is a Celtic deity associated with healing, the sea, hunting and dogs. He was worshipped in ancient Britain, most notably in a temple complex at Lydney Park in Gloucestershire, and possibly also in Gaul. He is equated with the Roman gods Mars, Mercury, Neptune and Silvanus, and his name is cognate with that of the Irish mythological figure Nuada and the Welsh Nudd.

Gods and Goddesses starting with O:

Ogmios was a Gaulish deity, who Lucian records was depicted as a bald old man with a bow and club leading an apparently happy band of men with chains attached to their ears from his tongue. This is thought by some scholars to be a metaphor for eloquence, possibly related to bardic practices. Lucian records that the Gauls associated him with Hercules, but his appearance on two defixiones from Austria suggests that he was also associated with Hermes in Eastern Celtic tradition. He is likely related to the Irish god Ogma, god of eloquence and runes and is one of the closest Gaulish parallels to Ogma's brother, the Dagda.

Ogma (Irish God): god of eloquence and runes.

Gods and Goddesses starting with R:

Robur was the god of oak trees, worshipped primarily in Gaul alongside Abellio, Fagus and Buxenus.

Rosmerta was a goddess of fertility and abundance in Gaul.

Rudianos was a war god worshiped in Gaul.

Gods and Goddesses starting with S:

Segomo ("victor, mighty one") was a war god worshipped in Gaul, and possibly in Britain and Ireland.

Senua was a Celtic goddess worshipped in Roman Britain. Senua's shrine may have been a ritual spring, into which offerings were thrown, surrounded by a complex of buildings including workshops and accommodation for pilgrims.

Sequana was the goddess of the river Seine, particularly the springs at the source of the Seine, and the Gaulish tribe the Sequani.

Sirona was a goddess worshipped predominantly in East Central Gaul and along the Danubian limes. A healing deity, she was associated with healing springs; her attributes were snakes and eggs. She was the sometimes depicted with Apollo Grannus or Apollo Borvo. She was particularly worshipped by the Treveri in the Moselle Valley.

Smertios or **Smertrius** was a god of war worshipped in Gaul and Noricum.

Sucellus or **Sucellos** was the god of agriculture, forests and alcoholic drinks of the Gauls.

Sulevia was a goddess worshipped in Gaul and Britain, very often in the plural forms Suleviae or Sule(v)is. Dedications to Sulevia(e) are attested in about forty inscriptions, distributed quite widely in the Celtic world, but with particular concentrations in Noricum, among the Helvetii, along the Rhine, and also in Rome.

Sul or **Sulis** (also found as Sulevis: see Suleviae) was the deification of spring-water, especially of thermal spring-water, conceived as a nourishing, life-giving Mother goddess. She is known especially from Bath, where she was worshipped as Sulis Minerva.

Gods and Goddesses starting with T:

Tailtiu is the name of a presumed Mother goddess from Irish mythology and the town in County Meath that was named after her.

Tamesis (British) was goddess of water, particularly fresh water.

Taranis was the god of thunder worshipped in Gaul and Britain and mentioned, along with Esus and Toutatis.

Toutatis or **Teutates** was worshipped in ancient Gaul and Britain. On the basis of his name's etymology, he has been widely interpreted to be a tribal protector.

Gods and Goddesses starting with V:

Verbeia was a goddess worshipped in Roman Britain. She is known from a single altar-stone dedicated to her at Ilkley. She is considered to have been a deification of the River Wharfe.

Vosegus was the patron god of the Vosges in eastern Gaul.

Gods and Goddesses starting with X:

Xulsigiae (Gaulish) were triple fertility goddesses worshipped at the healing-spring shrine in Augusta Treverorum (present-day Trier), a site also sacred to Mars Lenus. Clay figures of the Genii Cucullati have also been found at the same shrine.

Sources

www.godchecker.com

www.wikipedia.com

APPENDIX THREE
Personal Ritual Creation Worksheet

The Goal of this Ritual is:

Type of Ritual:

Worship | Sabbat | Esbat | Protection | Healing
Dedication | Devotional | Meditation | Visualization | Prayer
Divination | Rite of Passage | Self-Development
Other:

Select what you want to include in the ritual:

Common Parts of Ritual	Purpose in this ritual	Ideas on how to do it
Preparation / Setup		
Greetings / Welcome		
Cleansing / Smudging		
Cast Circle / Protections		
Invite / Call		
Building Energy / Focus		
Primary Ritual Act		
Offerings / Communion		
Thanks		
Grounding / Release		
Dissolve Circle / Protections		
Cleanup / Takedown		

Below are some checklists for the different parts of the Ritual to help figure out what you want to do:

Time and Place:	Preferred Choice	Reasons
Time of Ritual		
Date of Ritual		
Phase of Moon		
Weather		
Indoor or Outdoor / Where		
Physical Space Required		
Other:		

Cleansing / Smudging:	What / Why	How / With What
Pre-Ritual Cleansing (bath, diet, anointing, etc.)		
Cleanse Ritual Area		
Other:		

Cast Circle / Protections	What / Why	How / With What
Define ritual area		
Cast Magic Circle		
Create Other Defenses		
Personal Protections (amulets, stones, etc)		
Other:		

Invite / Call	Who / What to be called	Why calling them? What will they do?
God / Goddess / Deity		
Guardians		
Elements		
Ancestors		
Spirits		
Other:		

Energy to be used	What will it be used for?	How will it be used?	How will you build it?
Personal			
Divine			
Elemental			
Ancestors			
Planetary / Celestial			
Cosmic / Universal			
Other:			

How will energy be raised / focused / banished	What will it be used for?	How will it be used?	How will you build it?
Chant / Song			
Dance / Movement			
Meditation			
Guided Visualization			
Prayer			
Physical Movement (sweep, jump, crawl, hop, etc.)			
Music			
Drumming			
Other:			

Ritual Components / Tools	What kind(s)	How will it be used	Charge Before Ritual?
Athame / Sword / Blade			
Cup / Cauldron			
Candle			
Incense			
Feather			
Poppet / Voodoo Doll			
Rope / Ribbon			
Animals (claws, teeth, etc.)			
Elements (earth, water, etc.)			
Plants / Flowers / Herbs			
Oils / Essences			
Masks			
Bells / Gongs / Chimes			
Wand / Staff / Rings			
Other:			

Dissolving Circle / Protection	What techniques or tools will be used?	Special Notes
Taking Down / Opening Circle		
Releasing those Invited/ Called		
Thanking God / Goddess / Divinity		
Breaking Wards		
Cleaning Up (Mundane)		
Other:		

Resolution	What techniques or tools will be used?	How will it be used?	Special Notes
Energy Release			
Breakdown of Ritual Space			
Cleaning Up (Mundane)			
Other:			

Sketch Layout of Ritual Area and/or Altar:

```
   N
W + E
   S
```

After the ritual, complete this section to help you remember, refine and improve future rituals:

Details:	This Ritual	Notes for Future Rituals
Time of Ritual		
Date of Ritual		
Phase of Moon		
Weather		
Indoor or Outdoor / Where		
Physical Space Required		
Amount of "Involvement"		
Other:		

What were the memorable parts of the ritual for you?

What lessons were learned from this ritual?

Other Notes:

Appendix IV
Examples of Rituals

I'm going to start with a ritual that invokes the three realms and doesn't have circle casting. As with every ritual you first gather all your needed materials in one place and decorate your altar or Shrine with whatever decorations are appropriate for the occasion.

Start with purification: For this you will need a bowl of spring water or rainwater that has been left out in the moon at night to be blessed by the gods.

To purify your ritual tools: sprinkle them with the water and say "Be Pure" then dry them with a white towel.

To purify yourself: dip your hand into the water, touch your forehead and say: "May I be pure that I might cross through the sacred."

Dip your hand again, touch your lips: "May I cross through the sacred that I may attain the holy."

Dip your hand again, touch your heart and say: "May I attain the holy that I might be blessed in all things."

The Ritual: I'm going to use Samhain as an example for this ritual.

Once you and your altar/shrine tools are purified and the set up of your altar/shrine is complete the first step is to invoke the three realms. You sit or stand in front of your altar/shrine and say a blessing for the three realms. I'm going to give an example here but there are many different ones:

"The waters support and surround me.
The land extends about me.
The sky reaches out above me.
At the center burns a living flame."

Then light the main candle on your altar/shrine (this will serve as your hearth fire or main fire). And say:
"I light this fire to carry my prayers to the Gods of my ancestors."

Next you ask the Gods, nature spirits, and ancestors to join you and the gods you will be honoring specifically for this ritual.

"I ask the Gods of my ancestors to join me in my ritual, I ask my ancestors to guide me, and I ask the land spirits to aid me. I ask Lugh and An Morrigan to join me, I am your child."

As you call on each of them offer a bit of bread or oats to the sacred fire (the candle).

Next you state the purpose of the ritual: "I am here to celebrate the feast of Samhain, to honour my ancestors and my Gods and to ask blessing for the New Year."

Now it is time to make the **main offering to the Gods**. Pick up the offering to Lugh and raise it above your head, then say:

"To Lugh Lamfhada, I honour you. Samildananch, I offer you my hospitality! The Voice of Thunder, I give thanks for your blessings and protection!" Now place the offering for the place designated for Lugh. Next pick up the offering for An Morrigan and raise it above your head and say: "To An Morrigan, I honour you. My Queen, I offer you my hospitality and give thanks for your blessings and protecttion!" Now place the offering in the place designated for An Morrigan. Next do the same for the spirits of the land. "To the Spirits of this Land, I honour you!
To all Spirits of Rocks, Springs, and Mounds, I offer my respect! To all Spirits of the Green World and its Denizens I strive to be a good neighbour to you." And finally for your ancestors, recite the names of the ancestors you want to remember and say, "I remember and honour you and invite you to my feast."

Next is a time for **personal prayers** or any **seasonal customs** (from your country or the country you live in) that this may be a good time for.

"A New Year is born from you; praise blessings, and honours are due for this gifts! Hear my words, you who give birth to everything. A newly born year takes its place among your wonders, one more thing for which you might rightly be praised."

This would be the time to meditate or use divining tools. Then you thank the Gods, ancestors, and land spirits for coming to your ritual. Then you eat the food you brought with you and from which the offerings came. As you pack everything and clean up say: "As it was, as it is, as it evermore shall be."

The following is an Imbolc Ritual from NOD, it is geared towards a group but it can be adapted to individual use.

Items to be used: Take your Ribbon and a Pen (one that will work on the ribbon). Alternative is to turn all lights off in home for 5 minutes and light some candles.

N.O.D. Imbolc Chat Ceremony

Open ceremony

Ceremony leader:
I cast this circle around the homes of each here in. The many circles around the world are as one in this place. May no ill will or harm enter this circle in the names of our Gods, Goddesses and Ancestors.

Let the four directions be honoured that their energy and radiance might enter our circle in blessing.

Hail the Element of Earth in this Place of Winter. May there be peace in the North.
Hail the Element of Air in this Place of Spring. May there be peace in the East.
Hail the Element of Fire in this Place of Summer. May there be peace in the South.
Hail the Element of Water in this Place of Autumn. May there be peace in the West.

May there be peace in the entire world!

We who walk the path of old turned new are gathered in this place, to honour the changing of the seasons. On this day we celebrate in new ways told traditions of Imbolc - the return of long light filled days, days of renewal! We will offer peace in this place so there may be peace in all. We now speak the druid prayer.

All (one line at a time):
Awaken Gods, Goddesses all,
And hear our heartfelt earthbound call,
To see beyond what we can see,
To know the truth that lies with thee.
To know the truth of Earth's firm touch,
To feel the truth of the fires rush,
To breath the truth of rich clear air,
To drink the truth of water fair.

We ask for the solid strength of stone,
For warmth to heat our hearth and home,
We ask for the wisdom of the oak,
For food and water to feed all folk.
Please guide us down our chosen path,
So we may sing and dance and laugh,
And love and give and hope and dream,
To live the life that we have seen.

Celebration of ceremony

Ceremony leader:
  I call upon Bel, God of the Sun,
  and Arianhrod, Goddess of the Moon,
  I call upon Llyr, God of the Seas,
  and Brigid, Goddess of the Fires,
  I call upon Bran the Blessed, God of Prophecy,
  and Ceridwen, Goddess of Magic
  I call upon Afallach, God of the Otherworld,
  and Modron, Mother Goddess of us all,
  To witness this Sacred Ceremony,
  And bless us with your presence!

We come together this day of renewal of light and purification in a world of darkness. Life is new once more, young is nature and her gifts. We celebrate rebirth upon this blessed day!

All:
  We celebrate rebirth upon this blessed day!

Ceremony leader:
  We now take this opportunity to reflect for 5 minutes on what we would like to see Grow; in health and strength this year, for ourselves and for those around us. Feel free to also use this time to write key words or thoughts on the Ribbon for blessing from Bridget. Those of you who do not have a ribbon can light some candles and turn all the lights off for this time.

(We take 5 mins to reflect)

All (one line at a time):
  As the long night of Winter, comes to an end
  As the cold ground awakens from Winter sleep
  As the Sun awakens, rebirths
  We begin
  We celebrate rebirth upon this blessed day!

Ceremony leader:
  Is there any here who wish to share a prayer for the season?
  (if none continue to closing)
  As there are (none/no more) who wish to share a prayer for the season we will offer thanks and peace to those who have attended this rite with the druid prayer.

Close ceremony

All (one line at a time):
Awaken Gods, Goddesses all,
And hear our heartfelt earthbound call,
To see beyond what we can see,
To know the truth that lies with thee.
To know the truth of Earth's firm touch,
To feel the truth of the fires rush,
To breath the truth of rich clear air,
To drink the truth of water fair.

We ask for the solid strength of stone,
For warmth to heat our hearth and home,
We ask for the wisdom of the oak,
For food and water to feed all folk.
Please guide us down our chosen path,
So we may sing and dance and laugh,
And love and give and hope and dream,
To live the life that we have seen.

Ceremony leader:
I thank the Element of Earth and the powers of the North in this Place of Winter.

I thank the Element of Air and the powers of the East in this Place of Spring.

I thank the Element of Fire and the powers of the South in this Place of Summer.

I thank the Element of Water and the powers of the West in this Place of Autumn.

I thank the Gods and Goddesses for their presence and blessing in this ceremony.

I now unwind this circle in this place. As the one circle is the many circles around the homes of each here in, may they too be unwound.

Our celebration of the Imbolc festival has drawn to a close this day. You may now place your ribbon with a prayer outside, when you have the time, to be blessed by Bridget as she walks by this night with her light.

Hang your ribbon in a place you will see it daily. So that Bridget's blessings may be ignited as the Sun Grows.

May we leave with love and peace in our hearts for the seasons ahead!

Endnotes
Pagan Book of Prayers by Ceisiwr Serith

"By Ash, Oak, and Fir"

A Standard Outline for Druid Ritual in a Triad of Triads
by OakWyse

Ritual Outline

ASH (Arriving Phase)

Arrangements -

- Before the beginning of the ritual, the liturgical team prepares the Nemeton site, preparing the altar, and being sure that all tools, candles, offerings, etc. are in place.
- The Participants are briefed, and parts are assigned.
- Individuals do their personal meditations and preparations.

Setting the Mood -

(The purpose of the section is two-fold: to prepare the Participants for worship, and to establish the special mood and meaning of the particular celebration.)

- The ritual begins with a Musical Signal appropriate to the Celebration.
- The Participants process to the Nemeton.
- A Circle is cast, the directions/elements are invoked/honored
- A Worship Leader issues the Call to Worship, and the Participants respond with a unity chant appropriate to the season or the event.
- A Worship Leader asks for the Awen (Inspiration) to perform the ritual, stating the Ritual Purpose and Precedent, and Naming the Occasion and Deities.

Hallowings –

- A Worship Leader uses incense, smudge, water, or other purification to purify all Priests, other Worship Leaders, and all Participants.*
- The Participants are led in the Two Powers, Four Elements, Body of Light, or other Centering Meditation, or other observance to establish the Sacred Center.

(* A ritual preparation for worship. Humans are not naturally "impure," and do not need to be "purified" at each ritual.)

(At the conclusion of the Meditation, a Worship Leader moves to the center and prepares to honor the Earth Mother.)

OAK (Offering Phase)

Offerings and Omens -

- A Worship Leader offers a Prayer of Honoring to the Earth Mother, and offerings are made to Her.
- The Three Kindreds (Gods/Goddesses, Ancestors, Earth Spirits) are invoked by one or more Worship Leaders.
- Worship Leaders invoke the specific Deities of the Occasion.
- Praise Offerings, Dance, Libations, etc., are made
- Prayer of Acceptance opens the Participants to silent reflection on the Presence of those invoked.

Acceptings -

- Worship Leader leads the Participants in meditation on personal and group needs.
- An act of Reception is made for Blessings from Deities.
- Participants respond to Blessing with Consecration & Sharing of Waters of Life ("Cakes & Ale")

Kinetics (Workings) -

Now that the Power of Blessing has been given and received, optional workings or observances of the day or event may take place: spell casting, rites of passage, or other workings as needed.

(At the conclusion of the Workings, a Worship Leader moves to the center and begins the Thanksgivings of Farewell.)

FIR (Farewelling Phase)

Farewells -

Thanksgivings are offered to:
- Deities of the Occasion
- The Three Kindreds

Incantations -

- A song or chant is done in honor of Earth Mother
- Ending chant appropriate to the day or occasion
- Thanks to the directions, and unwinding of the circle

Retiring -

- An appropriate Musical Signal announces the End of the ritual.
- Procession from the Nemeton.

NOTES

The leader of the ritual (whether called Liturgist, Celebrant, Senior Druid, or other) assigns parts to each person present and briefs them on approximately what to say when their part comes up. At the appropriate time, the person is pointed to, and they do their part, and so the ritual flows.

The Blessings of the Gods and Goddesses be with you.

On Using Liturgy Sticks . . .

There is no historical evidence of the use of "Liturgy Sticks," but their function is certainly within the tradition of Celtic tree mysteries. Liturgy sticks are the tools and symbol of the Liturgist. They are three sticks about 1/2 inch by 18 inches made of ash, of oak, and of fir. Symbols for the names of the tree (in English, using Ogham, or Runes, or whatever) are marked on the respective sticks. They are carried in a bag, over the shoulder, when not in use.

In each phase the power and magic of the tree is added to the ritual and its participants. Liturgists may grasping the appropriate Stick for each phase, at the symbol on the stick for each of the three sub- phases. The sticks may be passed, like "talking sticks", to the person leading any part of the ritual. By learning these meanings for Ash, Oak, and Fir, and the basic contents of each part, any person can lead any ritual, even extemporaneously. And the format is a good guide to the discipline of ritual composition, whether it be solitary, family, small group, or large celebration. Its beauty lies in its simplicity.

APPENDIX V

A quick guide to the

Celtic Ogham

Birch

Birth and new beginnings. The continuing cycle of rebirth.

Rowan

Protection

Alder

Guidance, prophecy, and intuition.

Willow

The Moon, emotions, and witchcraft

Ash

Change, growth, and shape-shifting

Hawthorn

Obstacles, hostile forces, of complications

Oak

Endurance, strength, and maturity. Also nobility.

Holly

A test or challenge

Hazel

Wisdom, knowledge, and enlightenment

Apple

Health and healing, also rest and recouperation.

Vine

Harvest, celebration, and a successful finish to a task.

Ivy

The primal force of the survival instinct. Tenacity, ruthlessness.

Broom

Medicine or cleaning, especially in a purgative sense.

Blackthorn

Harm. Pain or wounding.

Elder

Regret, shame, or humiliation. The balancing of karma. May sometimes signify revenge.

Fir

Wonder, awe, or a heightened conciousness

Gorse

Sexuality, passion, eros

Heather

Lovers, partnership, or the bond of male and female

Poplar

A rite of passage. Coming to terms with one's own fear.

Yew

Death, an ending. Also gateways or the otherworld.

Overview of the modern Celtic Tree Calendar

	OGHAM NAME	TREE	CALENDAR	SONG OF AMERGIN
├	Beith	Birch	Dec 24 – Jan 20	*I am a stag of seven tines*
╞	Luis	Rowan	Jan 21 – Feb 17	*I am a wide flood on the plain*
╞═	Nion	Ash	Feb 18 – Mar 17	*I am a wind across deep waters*
╞≡	Fearn	Alder	Mar 18 – Apr 14	*I am the sun's bright tear*
╞≣	Saille	Willow	Apr 15 – May 12	*I am a hawk on a cliff*
┤	Huathe	Hawthorn	May 13 – June 9	*I am the beauty of the flowers*
╡	Duir	Oak	June 10 – July 7	*I am a god who puts fire in the head*
≡|	Tinne	Holly	July 8 – Aug 4	*I am a battle-keening spear*
≣|	Coll	Hazel	Aug 5 – Sep 1	*I am a salmon in the pool*
┼	Muin	Vine	Sep 2 – Sep 29	*I am the mountain full of poetry*
╪	Gort	Ivy	Sep 30 – Oct 27	*I am a strong wild boar*
╪≡	Ngetal	Reed	Oct 28 – Nov 24	*I am the roaring raging sea*
╪≣	Ruis	Elder	Nov 25 – Dec 22	*I am the wave of the sea*

Other Ogham dates in the calendar

	OGHAM NAME	TREE	CALENDAR
┼	Ailm	Silver Fir	Winter Solstice / Yule / Alban Arthuan (Dec 21)
╪	Onn	Furze	Vernal Equinox / Ostara / Alban Eiler (March 21)
╪≡	Ura	Heather	Summer Solstice / Litha / Alban Heruin (June 21)
╪≣	Eadha	Aspen	Autumn Equinox / Mabon / Alban Elued (Sep 21)
╪≣≣	Idho	Yew	Midwinter Eve (evening before Winter Solstice)

Appendix VI
Guide To Meditation

Meditation is used to relax the mind, to focus and train your mind to harness energies and ideas, which are around it. It allows people to gain control of their thoughts and emotions. It allows one to focus on a particular thought or emotion, helping to find answers in chaos and in peace.

Meditation can be used for spiritual enlightenment, helping people gain insight into themselves and their motivations. It can open one up to herself or himself and that which lies within.

Meditation can also help reduce stress, lower blood pressure, and aid in concentration. One does not have to be Religious or spiritual to benefit from meditation, although many faiths practice it as a way to get closer to the divine.

Allow yourself to open up to your natural rhythms and your natural pace. Don't force yourself into doing anything, which your body does not want to do. Do not over work yourself; even meditation can be strenuous.

Basic Meditation

Breathe slowly and deeply, keeping a steady rhythm and focus on your breath.

Relax, allow all tension to be released from every muscle in your body.

Try to control your heart rate through steady breathing. This will help reduce blood pressure and stress in your muscles.

Clear you mind. Try not to dwell on any one thought. If you have trouble with this, visualize a black screen. As thoughts come into your mind, just gently nudge them out. Try to focus your energies on melding into the earth. Attune yourself with the power and solidity, which resides within it. This is referred to as grounding. Picture the earth energies rising up around you while you root your own energies into the ground.

Focus your energies inward. Allow yourself to become one with them.

The Uses of Meditation

Meditation has many different uses and it can be applied into practically every aspect of your life.

Children do it naturally. Have you ever watched a child so absorbed in play that he isn't even aware of anything beyond his fascination with his toys? If someone were to walk up behind him, the child would be startled.

Meditation requires that you acquire this type of absorption. This absorption is what refreshes and heals.

Meditation is a very powerful tool. As our muscles relax, our mind will quiet down and our sagging spirits will revive. We are once again in control of our lives.

Scientific research has repeatedly proven that meditation has many great benefits such as:
- slowing down our aging process
- alleviating pain
- letting us get by on less sleep
- lowering our serum cholesterol level
- reducing bacteria levels in our saliva thereby fewer cavities
- increasing blood flow to brain making us smarter
- better memory
- plus many, many more benefits too numerous to mention

Everyone who meditates on a daily basis claims different benefits he or she acquired in these four levels: emotional -mental – physical - spiritual.